TRISH

Hope I'...

MW01493789

AND THE
BEAT
GOES ON

THE LIFE OF DONALD BEZAHLER

DONALD BEZAHLER
WITH KENT WALLACE

AND THE BEAT GOES ON
THE LIFE OF DONALD BEZAHLER

Published by Fig Factor Media, LLC.
Cover Design and Layout by Juan Pablo Ruiz
Printed in the United States of America

ISBN: 978-1-7345680-4-2

THIS BOOK IS DEDICATED TO MY BELOVED WIFE, MARY, AND MY CHILDREN, DAVE AND AMBER, WHO MADE THIS WHOLE STORY WORTHWHILE

CONTENTS

Don Bezahler was an ordinary Joe from Brooklyn, who put himself through Harvard on the GI Bill, achieved the highest level of professional success, became the legendary Dragon-Slayer, all the while attracting numerous conquests and marriages, and then eventually, and unwittingly, found unconditional, everlasting love.

PREFACE

Little did I ever think that I would want to put pen to paper to recall the more interesting parts of my life, nor did I believe that anyone would be interested in reading it. However, strange things happen when one is preparing for open-heart surgery, and Mary is insistent upon me doing this. If you know Mary like I know Mary, you know I would have no choice. She hired Kent Wallace to do the writing, and arranged for a publisher to publish it. Kent is a great writer and quite a character, and we hit it off. Kent is now in Vietnam, to finish his own novel and start his new adventure in life.

So here we begin the task of making my life a little more interesting, and hope the reader learns a little about the Don only I know so well. Hopefully, the people I refer to will share in my journey.

~ Donald Bezahler
Naples, FL. April 2020

Donald Jay Bezahler born April 10, 1932

FOREWORD
BY KENT WALLACE

When first asked to participate in the project, "And the Beat Goes On", I was thrilled. Perhaps even more so than the subject of the biography himself! Don would sit at the kitchen table, telling me his life story in bits and pieces and I would then return to my abode in Hollywood, Florida, and give these fragments definition and meaning.

But as time went on, Don's enthusiasm began to gather speed. So much so, that by the end of the project I reckon we hit the wire in a dead heat...

Since I was only a casual acquaintance of Mr. Bezahler when asked to author his biography, I was awed by the stories that streamed from Don's vast recollections. However, it was his honesty, his fearlessness to address failures and foibles, that caught me off guard. Don was an open book from start to finish.

In "And the Beat Goes On" Don often takes it on the chin. He holds nothing back—the good and the bad receive equal shrift.

Don's story is one of grandeur and success—million-dollar deals and clever business ploys (which sometimes backfired). But his tale is also one of personal redemption—very much a love story.

While the book is Don's biography, it is also the story of "Mary and Don" with special appearances by Asia (their four-legged family member).

Don bared his soul and allowed me a ringside seat on the roller-coaster ride of his life.

The fact that Don was diagnosed with a serious heart ailment while we were in midst of the project only added to the candidness of our conversations.

The book suddenly took on an almost improvisational vibe, forcing Don to not simply dwell on a life already lived, but on a life in the balance. The drama of those particular days created a deeper and more daring dive into self-introspection. Mere reminiscing was nudged into wistful reflection and the projection of what lay ahead.

The grandson of Jewish immigrants, Don rose to skyscraper status in the legal profession. And while there were failed marriages and a disenfranchised son (a wound which has since mended), this book is a candid, no-holds-barred, excursion in honesty.

Don's aorta has been repaired, and yet the Dragon Slayer's heart is very much exposed...

CHAPTER 1
THE SAGA BEGINS

"That moment on the corner, with a crowd, was the 'eye opener'
that motivated me."

~ Don Bezahler

Summer—Long Island, NY—1970's

Don Bezahler was hobnobbing, in a social way, with some neighbors in the Hamptons. He ran into one Jerry Burns (whom Don, of course, recognized as the renowned greeter and part owner of the iconic '21' Club).

Oddly, to Jerry, Don's last name offered even greater intrigue.

There's no doubt Don was aware his grandfather Louis was a "mensch" of the highest order. (*Mensch is a Yiddish word meaning a person of integrity and honor*).

Louis was a man immersed in the travails of the Eastern European Jewish migration that took place under the watchful gaze of Lady Liberty. Many of those families (like Don's) arrived, often hunkering down in Manhattan's Lower East Side.

Manhattan's Lower East Side, at that time, was teeming mostly with Jewish immigrants, seeking to make lives for themselves in the hustle and bustle of the City. There were pushcarts on every corner, selling wares like clothing, pickles, sauerkraut, and the like. Shopping was done at street level, while sellers of merchandise were seeking outlets for their wares.

Louis was very active in the Workmen's Circle (a society that helped members get started with their new lives in America), but Jerry added a few new twists, otherwise unbeknownst to Don. Don knew that Louis had the title of "Medical Director" although not a medical doctor. Apparently, Louis, above and beyond his aforementioned credits, also used his position to provide loans, usually without interest, to assist in bringing families from the "Old Country." And not only that, the mother of Jack Kriendler (the other part-owner of '21'), the most renowned mid-wife in New York City, in 1899 delivered Don's father Joel, the first in the family born in the United States. At that time it was not unusual for babies to be delivered at home, by midwives, rather than in hospitals.

*****

In the late 1800's, Don's family (father's side) arrived in New York from what was then Austria, now Poland, settling in the Lower East Side of Manhattan, eventually swapping Boroughs and moving to the Bronx before moving back to Brooklyn in 1932.

Mom's side of the family tethered up in the early 1900's, arriving from Poland, via Alexandria, Egypt, and also finding themselves in the Lower East Side of New York City.

Joel was the eldest of eight and Hannah (Don's mom) the eldest of a trifecta. The two would eventually meet at a social event sponsored by the Lower East Side's Patria Club.

Far from being children, Joel was twenty-six and a graduate of New York University, attending night school with a major in accountancy, while working full time. Hannah was a seventeen-year-old high school graduate and, despite the age difference, the pair clicked.

The budding Lower East Side lovebirds would meet on the streets and hang out on the stoops until one day Joel asked Hannah out on a proper date, marking the beginning of a two-year courtship which would culminate in nuptials.

At the time, Joel was working for Louis B. Mayer, while Hannah was a secretary to Artie Bulova, the president of the Bulova watch company. Once married, the couple moved to the Bronx, where Joel's family had relocated.

In short order, Hannah became pregnant and daughter Arline was born in March 1929. New York City passed London for the most populous urban area in the world, growing by almost 25 percent from 1920 into the 1930s. In 1929 the country entered the Great Depression, which lasted until 1939 and the onset of World War II.

"My sister dropped and so did the stock market," Don, with a grin, shrugged.

Despite the Depression, Don's father remained employed with Mayer and in 1932 Hannah was pregnant with Don. Joel then moved his brood to Brooklyn where Hannah's family had reassembled.

"The family's move to Brooklyn made sense in many ways, as my father was working in sales and distribution for MGM films. He was on the road a lot, and I suspect my mom wanted to be near her mother, especially with another child on the way," Don explained.

For a nice Jewish family, the births of both children had oddly Christian slants—Don was born on Palm Sunday in 1932 while his elder sister, Arline, was born on Easter Sunday in 1929.

"We've had a few chuckles on that coincidence over the years," Don smiled.

And while Don recalls the apartment his family lived in, riding his tricycle in the courtyard at 1320 51st Street, and joining his mother shopping for groceries on 13th Avenue, he has always considered 5200 15th Avenue, Brooklyn, his home.

Brooklyn, in the 1930s, was a borough consisting primarily of Italian, Irish and Jewish immigrants, living in separated residential areas, with a Jewish neighborhood, Italian neighborhoods, and Irish neighborhoods. Don's home was in the Jewish section of Brooklyn, known as Borough Park.

"In 1939 we moved into 5200 15th Avenue, a newer apartment building. We stayed until 1953. The most vivid memories of my youth are grounded there."

"In fact, I'd met a kid, my age, his name, Gerald Gould. Remember, this is going back to 1935. As fate would have it, both of our families moved into 5200 15th Avenue at the same time--we were in 3B and they were in 2B. To this day, Gerald and I call each other on birthdays, recently celebrating our 85th anniversary as friends," Don stated with nostalgic joy.

Don's youth was typical of the times; one of school, softball, stickball and pitching pennies. There were trips to Ebbets Field where he'd watch his favorite Brooklyn Dodger Dixie Walker roam the outfield. On sweltering summer nights, Don recalls sleeping on the fire escape. Obviously, there was no air-conditioning at the time. His youth was one of family and neighborhood first.

But Don had dreams, and as far back as he could remember, he desired a career in law. That fate was sealed when, as a 10-year-old, he gave an impassioned street-corner speech for incumbent Mayor William O'Dwyer who was up for re-election.

"I could always talk, maybe better with my mouth than with a stick-ball bat," he said with a smile, adding, "That moment on the corner, with a crowd, was an eye-opener. It motivated me. It's not as though my family was wanting, we got by, but for me that simply wasn't enough. At a very early age I knew I wanted more. I wanted to excel both financially and socially, and once I realized that I had a gift, I felt nothing could hold me back."

CHAPTER 2
HOME FROM THE WAR

"My father was mild mannered...it was my mother...who provided discipline around the house."
~ Don Bezahler

June 1955—A Random Gin Joint—Brooklyn, NY

Don Bezahler had recently returned from his Korean War stint, moved back into his parents Brooklyn apartment, and was plotting his future—leaning toward law and an education at an Ivy League school.

Don's not a big drinker, but he'll imbibe on occasion. His father, Joel, on the other hand, is a teetotaler. Always the breadwinner, but not much of an in-house influence, Joel accompanied his son to these elbow bending sessions—he simply refused to leave his son alone at such a pivotal time in the lad's life.

*****

Talk about dodging a bullet, Don's father received his draft notice on November 12, 1918, the day after the Armistice Treaty was signed. But it wasn't simple luck that would define Joel Bezahler, rather a healthy work ethic.

"My father was a saint. I suspect that being the eldest of eight children provided him an early sense of familial responsibility," Don said. "He earned his degree at NYU, but he did so by going to night school so that he could work days to help provide for his parents and siblings—that's just the way he was. Ironically, he received a degree in accountancy, but never applied it. Instead, he landed a job with Louis B. Mayer and never looked back."

Joel worked sales, finding outlets (movie houses) for Mayer-produced films. Once Mayer partnered with Samuel Goldwyn (forming MGM), Joel opted to stay in New York—continuing his sales shtick rather than moving to Hollywood and working production with the fledging, soon to become, movie-making empire.

"In my father's case, luck did raise its head again when the Depression hit. You see, one application that sustained throughout the Great Depression was entertainment, and especially films," Don recalled. "My father garnered a weekly paycheck. As a result, our family never felt the starvation conditions so many others faced during that dark period. Many had lost everything—my father was an unwavering breadwinner throughout."

Don's mom, Hannah Goldberg, was also born in New York. She parlayed her high school education into a career in stenography, finding secretarial work once she graduated.

The couple, who knew each other from the neighborhood, married in 1927.

Don pointed out, "There was a nine-year age difference when they wed. My father was twenty-eight, my mother nineteen, and at that time the age difference was significant."

But that wasn't the only gap between the two lovebirds. Don said, "My father was mild mannered—serene. It was my mother, not my dad, who provided discipline around the house. She was the one who made sure we did our homework and chores, and all of those sorts of things."

"I recall dad coming home each evening at 6 p.m. Dinner was always served, promptly at 7 p.m. That is, when my father wasn't on the road, which he frequently was, working for MGM."

"My father's vice, if you want to call it that, was going to the track—either Belmont or Aqueduct, on Saturday. He'd often take me along. My parents were opposites in so many ways, and perhaps that was their attraction—they made a wonderful team."

"When I returned from (war) duty, and before I started at Harvard, my dad, who didn't drink, would join me. He was my friend at a crucial time in my life. I suspect he didn't want me to go it alone. He was there for me—a rock."

"My mom was another story. She was a tough, no-nonsense, play-it-by-the-book type. My elder sister Arline and I towed the line, I more so than Arline."

Tragedy struck when Don was eleven. A sister, Vicki Mae, was born. She died of medical complications at 10 months of age.

"It was certainly a turning point in the dynamics of our household," Don said. "Tension, dread, and irritability sort of consumed my mother—she worked through a long and strenuous mourning process. Despite the emotional swings, Mom never shirked her role—she'd still help me with my homework and handled the daily responsibilities of the house, while my dad remained an indefatigable breadwinner."

Don credits his father's work ethic for much of his personal motivation.

"My father toiled. Don't get me wrong, he loved what he did but the most money he ever made was $15k in a year. I used to make that in a week," Don pointed out. "I believe that irony instilled in me the desire to truly excel. For instance, I made sure my son had the opportunity to attend private schools, to provide tangible benefits for my family that my father couldn't, but not for lack of trying."

Joel worked until he was seventy-years old. He retired with a modest pension—having remained with MGM throughout. Joel and Hannah moved from Brooklyn to Long Beach in Nassau County, where Don, now a super successful and caring son, provided whatever his parents needed or desired.

In 1979 Joel passed at the age of 80, a ripe old age in the 1970's. Joel had suffered from congestive heart failure for many years, and he ultimately succumbed to this condition.

"My mother remained in the Long Beach apartment until I recognized that time was catching up with her. By now I was spending a lot of time in Miami and I felt she ought to be closer, so I could be helpful to her needs," Don remembered. "I moved her into a quaint Deerfield Beach apartment and visited weekly, bringing food, or whatever, she needed. At some point it became obvious that my mom required full-time care, so I moved her into a nursing home."

Of course, like so many spirited elders, Hannah resisted the move. Don eased the transition by moving her bed and many other items from the Deerfield Beach pad into her new digs in the nursing home.

"I'll never forget the day we made the move," he said. "An old man (a resident) was seated in the lobby. He looked me square in the eye and said, 'They beat us here.' It appeared nothing more than a non sequitur, but it also seemed a somehow ominous statement."

"I received a call that my mother had fallen out of her bed and was sent to the hospital. The doctors were skeptical, explaining that the injuries did not appear the result of falling from a bed."

With Don prepared to strike a lawsuit, the nursing home quietly rushed a check—an unfulfilling and tacit acknowledgment of their malfeasance. Hannah, though, never left the hospital, passing away at the age of 93.

His parents are buried beside one another in Mount Hebron Cemetery in Flushing, New York, along with baby Vicki Mae.

CHAPTER 3
FORMATIVE YEARS – A MAN WITH A PLAN

"We weren't poor, but we didn't have the luxuries of many others in the neighborhood."
~ Don Bezahler

1944—Montauk Junior High School

Don Bezahler has always been a man with a plan, even when he was a kid. On a day, back in '44, he and his best bud were thinking about cutting school. Rather than risk the wrath of both school administrators and parents by simply not showing up, Don hatched a plan.

It was a rainy day. In fact, it was pouring and so, Don reckoned, if the duo walked the ten blocks, moving slowly in the elements, hitting a puddle or two along the way, they would arrive at school soaked to the bones.

And that they did. As a result, they were promptly sent home.

That, my friend, is cutting school Don Bezahler style...

*****

From 1937 through 1943 Don attended PS 103 in Brooklyn, despite a move from 49th Street to 52nd Street during that period.

"It was a fairly pedestrian experience," he said. "I'd walk to school, come home for lunch at noon—my mom always prepared a hot, solid, well-rounded meal—and afterwards I'd play punch-ball and stick-ball in the streets, until the sun went down. I was a good student, and I seemed to come by it naturally, without a great deal of effort."

PS 103 led to Montauk Junior High and despite the antidote, Don was far from a truant, rather a dedicated student with something of a mission in mind.

When Don was 11-years old his mother gave birth to a third child (Don had an older sister). "We weren't poor, but we didn't have the luxuries of many others in the neighborhood. We had no car or television, and I vividly recall wondering how another mouth to feed would affect my existence. It was a bit of a self-serving thought but not outlandish for a kid. My fears would never materialize."

"My baby-sister died at 10 months of age. The trauma rattled me to the core. A sense of guilt was followed by a burning desire to excel, to change my station in life, to truly make something of myself."

It was during this period that Don began writing poetry about subjects such as puppy love dashed, the lingering war (WWII), and the death of a sister.

Don shared two stories that seemed to stick out in his

mind during this period of youth. In one instance, his friend's cousin, Roberta Peters, made an operatic splash at the Met.

"It was quite exciting. Roberta filled in for Diva Nadine Connor, who had taken ill only six hours before the curtain call. Roberta was tasked with performing in Don Giovanni. She was a smash hit and the toast of the town! It felt good—that vicarious rush of being part of sudden success," Don said. The rest is history at the Met. Roberta went on to become the star of the Metropolitan Opera House for many years to come.

Then there was Don's Bar Mitzvah. While not a particularly religious family, Don felt that he ought to honor his Jewish faith, just as the other kids in the neighborhood had.

"I really didn't want to go to Hebrew School," he said, "So my father arranged for the Rabbi to tutor me privately. I caught on quickly and had my Bar Mitzvah. The kicker was that my mother's cousin owned a bar & grill in downtown Manhattan that was frequented by legendary boxer Rocky Graziano, and that's where my party was held. For a poor kid from Brooklyn, it was quite a splash."

Don was gearing up for high school as the war was winding down. "I used to listen to the radio every evening and I recall the newscaster, Gabriel Heatter, signing off each night by saying, 'We're one day closer to peace.' Indeed, the war did end when my high school sojourn began."

Don was enrolled at New Utrecht in Brooklyn where he rode the subway to and from school. "I recall a certain amount of jealousy. Many of my friends were in private schools; they could afford the luxury. Again, I believe my reality prompted me to excel, to strive—I knew I'd improve my station in life. It was my quest."

When it was time for college, Dartmouth seemed to be high on the list for Don's friends, and he recalls the stinging rejection when his application for enrollment was turned down while one of his buddies was accepted.

"I knew I had every bit the grades and skills as this particular fellow," Don recalled with a bit of heat. "The difference, I suspected, was that he'd gone to a fancy private high school, whereas I'd gone to public. That was it for me. I decided right then and there that I would go to a public college, work my ass off, and then get accepted by all the top law schools!"

So, Don enrolled in Brooklyn College with free tuition. He lived at home and excelled on the debate team and the Latin club. He kicked butt on his exams and after graduation aced the LSAT (Law School Admission Test). He then applied to Harvard, Yale, and Columbia Law Schools and was accepted by them all!

But the Korean War, which had been underway during his college days (thus a deferment at the time), was not as understanding. Ivy League law schools weren't the only ones who wanted Don—Uncle Sam was wagging his finger and law school would have to wait.

CHAPTER 4
THE RETURN OF MARIELLA

*The couple never spoke or wrote or communicated in
any fashion for the next thirty years.*
~ according to Don Bezahler

1980—Ritz Hotel—London

The phone rang in the suite occupied by Don Bezahler and his then-wife, Suzanne. Don answered. The voice at the other end stated quite simply, "This is Mariella..."

Yes, Mariella, Don's first true love. Mariella, the Austrian chanteuse who seduced the young soldier back in 1953. The "older woman" who taught the GI how to live daring, attend the opera, eat and drink in style, and even indulge in manicures.

For nearly 30 years there was nary a letter—absolutely no communication at all between the two until that trip to London. When a sixth sense—an uncanny vibe of Mariella's presence overwhelmed Don—and the game was afoot.

*****

In 1953, in what would prove to be the waning days of the Korean War, the government of the United States was still drafting 80,000 American youth per month.

Twenty-one-year-old Don Bezahler, a lad with plans of attending Harvard Law School, decided to take a proactive route. "I went to the draft board seeking a deferment so I might attend law school. Unfortunately, the board told me that a one-year deferment was the best I could expect. That didn't sit well, so I refused and a week later I received my notice."

Don's basic training took place at New Jersey's Fort Dix. "When I was issued my orders, I was told I'd be serving with the USFA. Frankly, I thought the "A" stood for Alaska and I wanted no part of that. Keep in mind, at the time Alaska wasn't a state but rather an outpost. In my opinion, Alaska was as removed as Outer-Mongolia. I went to my Commanding Officer and volunteered for duty in Korea."

Needless to say, Don's C.O. was aghast, advising the lad that the USFA was the best card you could draw in the deck— that he'd be serving with the United States Forces in Austria!

{Author's note: The reason for a U.S. military presence in Austria at the time was a result of Austria never having signed a peace treaty after WWII. Therefore, the country and Vienna we're divided into three zones: Russian, British, and American.}

Don shipped out on the USS Hodges, arriving in the port town of Livorno, Italy. On his first night the troops were treated to a live show—the young girl singing was Sophia Loren, prior to her breakout Hollywood movie career.

He was soon transferred to St. Johann in the Pongau province of Austria where he took a reconnaissance role with the 3rd Army Tank Corps. Ironically for the Jewish boy from

Brooklyn, they were housed in the former barracks of German SS troops.

Don served as a communications expert, driving the Company Commander. Their mission, if it should come to it, was to be prepared, in case of a Russian invasion, to blow up the mountain pass which was separated from the Russian zone by a mere path. Fortunately, it never came to that, but there was one harrowing moment.

During Don's first leave (a few months into his active service in Austria) and thanks to a contact of his father's, Don traveled to the Russian sector of Vienna. He was pleasantly surprised when the "family friend" turned out not to be an "old" couple, but rather a man in his 40's, Wolfgang Wolf, and his 31-year-old wife, the aforementioned Mariella.

Don became intoxicated, infatuated, and utterly inspired by Mariella, who seemed to take a keen interest in Don as well. That was the start of their relationship.

Don made frequent trips back to Vienna and Mariella, whether on leave or not, and she took him under her wing. Once she brought him to a party honoring an American General. Don, an enlisted man, was fairly terrified. After all, this soirée was for dignitaries and Generals—he was not supposed to be there. Fortunately, no one was the wiser and everything went off without a hitch.

On another occasion, Mariella brought Don to a Gasthaus (a German-style tavern and restaurant) in the woods of Vienna—the problem was that the Gasthaus was on the

Russian side.

Again, Don was a bit queasy about being found out. You see a U.S. soldier out of uniform could be arrested as a suspected spy. With a busload of Russian soldiers getting ready to enter the place, Don finally prevailed upon Mariella to leave, and she reluctantly agreed.

In 1955, with Don's two-year stint coming to an end, and with Austria finally signing that long-awaited treaty, it was time to leave. The couple never spoke or wrote or communicated in any fashion for the next 30 years. And that's where the Ritz comes in.

You see, in 1980, when Don and his wife were in London, Don had what might be best described as a premonition. He had an eerie inkling that Mariella was in London, and he simply had to satisfy the itch.

Don began by scouring the phone book where he found an M. Wolf. He called but could only leave the following message: "You may think this is a crazy call, but if you were in Austria, living in Vienna 30 years ago, this is Don and I need you to call me."

Days passed without a response and then on Saturday morning, the day before Don was to leave, that call came.

Oh, how they got along and reminisced (a planned dinner was quickly forgotten in the wash of rekindled spirits). The pair remained friends until Mariella's death, meeting often in New York on her bi-annual visits when Suzanne was out of town.

Such was the intimacy of their friendship, that Mariella bequeathed Don two drawings he'd long admired by the famous English sculpture/artist John Flaxman.

Meanwhile, back in Austria (1955), with the treaty signed and Don to soon depart (he would have gladly re-enlisted to stay near Mariella), the mood got dark. The Austrians who had been so accommodating to U.S. forces were now quite nationalistic (singing German war songs in the taverns) and the barroom brawls were epic.

"There was a saying," Don said with a laugh. "We didn't have to fight our way into Austria, but we had to fight our way out!"

There is a tragic irony in this chapter of Don's life. At the request of another soldier, who was going home in a few short days, Don and he swapped assignments.

This fellow had never experienced the recon-route along the Danube (a soldier would start at Linz, Austria and wind up in Passau, Germany, returning the following day).

Somewhere along the route the jeep the fellow was being driven in was hit by an arbitrary long-range weapon assumed fired by a Russian across the river. The jeep careened out of control and tumbled off a cliff, killing the kid who had taken Don's place that day.

It could have been Don being fished out of the swampy banks of the Danube, but it wasn't, and he returned to the States a short time later, suffering nothing more than a broken heart.

CHAPTER 5
SUBSIDIZING THE GI-BILL

"I recall the shrink telling me that I'd never make it ... I turned to him and said, 'You want to bet?'"
~ Don Bezahler

1955—Harvard Law School—Cambridge, MA

Don Bezahler is engaged in a poker game in his dorm at Harvard Law School. Don tends to head up these random games (daily) and he tends to clean up as well.

You see, Don has just returned from his Korean War stint, while most of his peers at Harvard are simply recently graduated college students.

Poker in the Army is like marching in the Army, and so you might say, Don has the upper hand.

In any event—Don Bezahler subsidizes his GI-Bill with pots from a poker table with a bunch of highly educated, well-heeled, greenhorns at one of the country's top law schools.

*****

"In August of 1955 I arrived at Harvard for orientation in my brand-new Plymouth, ready for a new chapter in my life. And while I wasn't entirely sure law school was the route I wanted to take. I'd decided to give it a shot," Don commented. "Since I hadn't made living arrangements in advance, I checked into a local hotel and decided to weigh my options. I was hopeful to get a space in the dorms."

{Author's Note: Don's law school ambitions had been interrupted by his call to serve in the U.S. Army, and while he'd been accepted to Harvard's school of law—he had to reapply after his tour—he was accepted once again.}

Don was the proverbial "fish out of water," as his veteran status stood in stark contrast of the majority of the "civilian" students.

He said, "Ironically, a former Lieutenant of mine from Austria was also entering at the same time. We weren't friends though, so I was pretty much on my own. It really was a bit of an awkward situation. I'd been in the Army, had lived in Europe and had been indoctrinated into the ways of the world, by Mariella, my worldly, older, paramour. Suddenly, I felt surrounded by children. People I had very little in common with."

Don worked out his dorm living arrangements, but it wasn't long before he realized that he'd need to supplement his GI Bill funding. A job was out of the question as law school studies are a full-time endeavor if you wish to excel. And that's how the poker games came into play.

"I was older than these guys, had vastly more real-world experience, including poker acumen. That's not saying they weren't a talented lot. In fact, one fellow went on to become the Attorney General of Rhode Island," he said with a chuckle.

Part of the process at Harvard Law included a psychological examination and while Don's wasn't particularly positive, it most certainly motivated him in ways the mere experience of being at Harvard hadn't.

"I recall the shrink telling me that I'd never make it. He claimed I had a lack of desire. I turned to him and said, 'You want to bet?'"

In the second year of the program, Don met Stan Strauss, a fellow who would play a significant role, if not in Don's professional career, most certainly in his love life.

"Frankly, I had little motivation outside of proving the headshrinker wrong," he remembered. "I simply couldn't relate to the co-ed's or townies (slang term for locals). I suspect I was still savoring the Mariella experience and perhaps still pining for her. I was also on a sort of intellectual cruise control. I wasn't aiming for A's, rather, quite satisfied, with a steady diet of B's—which I could accomplish with ease. In fact, during my entire stint at Harvard I never received a grade lower than a B. Conversely, I never received an A. However, I did come close."

{Author's Note: In the numeric grading world, a seventy-five was the equivalent of an A and Don received a seventy-four in Constitutional Law. He asked the professor to re-evaluate his score—it remained unchanged.}

Don's *laissez-faire* scholastic attitude carried over into summer breaks as well. He noted, "Most of my fellow classmates made a point of taking on internships with law firms during the summer—working on their end game. I became a rifle instructor at a children's summer camp in New England."

In Don's third and final year at Harvard, he hunkered down a bit. He recognized he had to ace the bar exam—which he did on his first shot! But let's go back...

"Law firms from everywhere would converge on the campus, interviewing second and third year prospects—it was part of the process, especially with Harvard being one of the, if not the, premiere law school in the country," he explained.

"What I learned early, however, was that they weren't necessarily looking for Jewish students. There was a certain anti-Semitic thread that ran through the 'White-Shoe' Wall Street firms with their 'Blue-Chip' clientele."

That said, Don did catch the eye of one Ned Gadsby, an Eisenhower appointee named to lead the U.S. Securities and Exchange Commission (SEC) in Washington, D.C.

"We hit it off. Ned sort of took me under his wing. He offered me a job once I graduated. I passed the bar exam in New York and went straight to work for the SEC!" Don's "B" status had landed him a starting role on an "A" Team lineup.

CHAPTER 6
TIME FOR A REAL JOB

Despite the fashion faux pas Don got the gig...

1958-1959—Securities and Exchange Commission—Washington, D.C.

Don Bezahler strode into the offices of the SEC at 125 F Street NW, full of confidence. And why not? The Harvard Law School graduate was already employed at the SEC, he had recently married his sweetheart Norma (his first wife), and now he was interviewing for the plum and powerful position of legal assistant to one of the commissioners, a Republican from New York.

Don was well prepared for the interview as he settled into his seat. As always, he was confident, borderline cocky.

And that's when he glanced down at his feet and noticed for the first time that he was wearing one brown shoe and one black shoe.

Despite the fashion faux pas Don got the gig...

*****

In 1957, during Don's second year of law school, his

suitemate, Stan Strauss, was getting married and the wedding was to take place in New York City. At the wedding a fetching young woman caught Don's attention. The fly in the ointment, however, was that Norma was engaged to the cousin of the bride-to-be.

During a dance, the bold, would-be barrister, told Norma, 'If you ever break your engagement look me up!'

Don then said, "I got a call from my sister in early 1958. She was a teacher in Brooklyn, New York, and she called to tell me there was an intern working with her who said she had met me at a wedding, and that she was no longer engaged. It was Norma, of course, and a grand case of kismet."

Needless to say, Don gave Norma a call, and on his next trip to New York he took her on a date.

"I graduated from Harvard in 1958 and took the New York Bar Exam. As a result, I traveled frequently to the city and was able to spend quite a lot of time with Norma."

In the summer of 1958 Don moved to Washington where he began working for the SEC, specifically in the Corporate Reorganization Group that was involved in Chapter 10 & 11 of the Bankruptcy Act. The not-so-long-distant relationship carried on, with Don making frequent trips to New York to visit his gal.

In 1959 Don was sent to Miami to represent the SEC in a vigorous bankruptcy case. He would ultimately spend two months, on and off, in The Magic City.

"The local attorneys were not at all happy with a

carpetbagger from the SEC being involved in their case," he noted. "I recall the leader of the Miami Bankruptcy Bar saying, 'This young punk from Washington comes to Florida to try and tell us what to do!' He said this in open court, in front of the judge."

But the judge didn't budge, and Don remained on the case. The *Miami Herald* carried the headline "SEC Lawyer Prevails in Ludman Case."

And in yet another instance of kismet, some twenty-years later, when Don moved to Miami's Towers of Quayside, it turns out the disparaging attorney was also a resident. The pair became good friends.

In March of 1959 Don and Norma were married and living in Washington, D.C., and that's when the opportunity for advancement at the SEC occurred. "This was a very potent position. You must understand there were only five commissioners and only five assistants—I was one of those assistants."

Despite the family's good fortune, Norma was miserable. She didn't like Washington, and she missed her family—a serious malaise had set in. "Moving was simply not an option. Frankly, I loved the D.C. lifestyle, and I had a powerful position. What we ultimately decided was that we ought to start a family. A child might assuage Norma's depression."

THE FAMILY GROWS

It was a day like any other day. May 3rd, 1961. Don and Norma were living in Brooklyn, on Ocean Parkway. Don got up and took the subway to work. He was then working at the SEC in New York. He was at the office for a couple of hours when he received a call that Norma was in real pain and he had to come home. He got into a town car and raced home.

Norma had decided that she would give birth by way of hypnosis, and each time she went to the doctor, she and Don would practice hypnosis, which worked well, and again, they practiced when they got home. However, neither of them contemplated that hypnosis would be impossible when Norma was in pain. It did not work, and they rushed her to the hospital. Norma gave birth, under a spinal injection. That was when their son, David, was born. He was 21 inches long and weighed seven pounds, nine ounces.

It was a memorable day for another reason. Don's mother, Hannah, came to the hospital, and when she got there, she walked into a glass door. Don spent some time in the emergency room with his mother, and in the delivery room with Norma. Finally, after a few days they brought David home.

Unfortunately, for Don and Norma things did not get better in their marriage, and when David was 16 months old, they decided to separate and would ultimately get a divorce.

Seeing David as he was growing up was difficult, but Don would arrange to see him for a few hours every weekend when he was in town, and when he was not in town, he would fly to Cincinnati where Norma and her then husband, had moved.

Things between David and Don were not good while he was growing up because Norma was insistent upon alienating the relationship. Norma had tried to change David's name to her married name, Price, while they were living in Cincinnati, to which Don objected strenuously. Don did the best he could under the circumstances, but it reached a crescendo when David was about to get Bar Mitzvahed.

Although Don continued to pay for everything for his child, he was told by David that he would prefer him not to attend the Bar Mitzvah. Don realized that this was Norma talking and not David, so he decided to go to temple with his current wife, Suzanne. It was a very bad situation, since nobody in the temple, including the rabbi, recognized Don as the father of David during the ceremony.

This changed however after his Bar Mitzvah. Suzanne had suggested that the family take a trip to Africa on a safari for David's 13th birthday, so David and Don, since Suzanne had backed out, went on safari and had an incredible time. When they got back, David turned to his father and said, "I wish we were first starting, rather than ending this wonderful trip."

After that, the relationship between Don and his son progressed in every conceivable way, mostly with the help of Mary, Don's wife and soulmate, and today they have the most incredible relationship. David, his wife Amber, and Don are very close, although the children now live some 3,000 miles away.

*****

Their son David was born on May 3rd, 1961. However, in November of 1960 John Fitzgerald Kennedy beat out Richard Nixon for the presidency of the United States. Ironically, in 1934 it was JFK's father Joseph who was named by FDR as inaugural chairman of the SEC.

When Kennedy took office in January 1961, the commissioner whom Don worked for was forced to resign. Suddenly, Don had no position, though he was still under the employ of the SEC.

"Another commissioner suggested I move to the New York office. To be frank, he had a motive. He wanted to have a finger on the pulse of the happenings there. I would report directly to this commissioner—and no one was to be the wiser. So, while I became just another attorney on the New York staff, I was also a spy!"

Needless to say, Norma was thrilled. But the move also allowed Don to follow up on a chit from the one-time Attorney General of New York, Nathaniel Goldstein. Don had met Goldstein in Washington and was told "If you ever move to New York look me up."

"We made the move and shortly thereafter I called on the former attorney general to ask about a position in the firm of Goldstein, Judd and Gurfein," Don said.

"At the time the firm employed 16 lawyers, eight Jews and eight Christians, and not by coincidence. In any event I met with General Goldstein who introduced me to the other partners. I recall a sit-down with Murray Gurfein, which was also attended by top-tier partner, Burt Abrams. The two were discussing something of a legal issue and I jumped in, disagreeing with Abrams perspective. Abrams mulled it over and told me that he suspected I was right. Murray exclaimed, 'You're the first lawyer that Burt Abrams ever admitted being wrong to.' I was offered a job on the spot!"

Don's ninety-day stint with the SEC in New York was soon to end and a new adventure about to begin. And when asked by the partners of Goldstein, Judd and Gurfein where Don saw himself in five-years, he replied, "In five years I expect to be a name partner."

"You mean a partner," he was corrected.

"No, I mean a *name* partner." And that's precisely what Don ultimately became.

Bursting with excitement, when Don returned home to Norma and gave her the good news, she asked how much Don would be earning. He didn't know. He hadn't asked. And she admonished him for taking a job without knowing how much he'd be paid. Don's bubble was only momentarily burst.

"When I started a few weeks later I mentioned to General Goldstein that we hadn't discussed remuneration. He asked about my then current salary with the SEC and I told him I was making $10,500 a year. General Goldstein suggested I start there. I was agreeable, but as always, I had to get in the last word. I told him I would take the matching salary, but at the end of my first year, I expected him to give me a check for what he felt I was worth—a bonus of sorts."

At the end of that first year General Goldstein presented Don with a check for another $10,500.

Despite Don's professional upward spiral, the marriage to Norma was on the rocks. And in November of 1962 they were divorced, with Norma and David remaining in Brooklyn, while Don moved to Manhattan.

CHAPTER 7
INTERNATIONALISM BECKONS

The once ten-year-old kid who stood on a Brooklyn street corner had made the international stage in the noblest of ways.

2005—Hilton Tel Aviv—Israel

For many years Don Bezahler worked for the high-powered New York law firm of Goldstein, Judd and Gurfein.

Nat Goldstein had been the Attorney General, Orrin Judd had been Solicitor General, and Murray Gurfein had been Chief Prosecutor, all under Tom Dewey when he was Governor.

The firm was involved with the about-to-be-recognized state of Israel (1948). President Harry Truman wanted to be the first to recognize Israel but also wanted Republican support, specifically the approval of Thomas Dewey who was then the head of the Republican Party. Using Goldstein, Judd and Gurfein was a natural.

Some years later, Don and his third wife, Mary, were in Israel attending a function with representatives of the Ministry of Finance. Mary was seated beside a high-ranking official. The official turned to Mary and stated, very matter-of-factly, "When you married Don Bezahler, you married the State of

Israel!"

Such was the significance of Don and his more than 40-year relationship with the nation of Israel.

*****

As previously stated, in 1961 Don joined the law firm of Goldstein, Judd and Gurfein.

Israel was a client. Yep, the government of Israel was a client of the firm--after all, the firm had played a significant role in the United States acceptance of the newly formed state.

Don was handed the responsibility of working with the Ministry of Finance of Israel and the Israel Bond Organization.

"I was Jewish, but I had no particular interest in Israel at the time as I had no significant religious or partisan leanings. The relationship simply began as a job," he said.

It wasn't long, however, before Don's involvement in the rapidly-growing nation expanded. He became involved in the building of the Tel Aviv Hilton Hotel and raising funds publicly for the Israel Bank of Agriculture, the Industrial Bank of Israel, as well as working for the Tourist Industry Development Corporation.

"Through my tasking I became acquainted, and held a close relationship, with the Minister of Finance, Levi Eshkol, who would later become the Prime Minister," Don pointed out.

Before long 40 to 50 percent of Don's time was spent on Israeli affairs. At the time there was an Arab nation blockade of Israel. Israel was bent on breaking the blockade and a plan was hatched.

"The powers that be in Israel figured that if they could perhaps build a world-class destination hotel utilizing the Hilton brand, similar to the Nile Hilton in Cairo, that might kick-start the dialogue."

The strategy didn't sit well with Egyptian leader Gamal Abdel Nasser, the second President of Egypt. Don explained, "Apparently Nasser, upon learning of the plan, promptly called Conrad Hilton, threatening to kick the Hilton out of Cairo if he went through with the Israeli program. Conrad called his bluff."

Nasser was more bluster than bravado. The hotel was built and soon became the most successful hotel in the Hilton chain.

On June 5, 1967, the start of the Six-Day War, the Minister of Finance beckoned Don, who--within days--was on a plane, arriving on the final day of the imbroglio (June 10th). If Don hadn't previously felt a binding attachment to his heritage and religion, he did then.

"I was put up in the Intercontinental Hotel in Jerusalem (previously off-limits to Jews) owned by Jordan and Pan American Airlines. I was the first Jew to stay in this hotel, in this holiest of cities," he recalled.

Jerusalem had been opened, for the first time in ages, to all (including Jews) and in a fairly grotesque, but otherwise celebratory moment, Don and fellow Jews were allowed to view the cobbled walkway leading to the Intercontinental Hotel which was paved with the headstones of pilfered Jewish gravesites.

During the period of the Six-Day War, Israel was in dire need of selling bonds in the United States. In order to accomplish this, they needed to have the bonds registered with the SEC in Washington. Don was put in charge of the task. Not only did he secure $300 million dollars in offerings, but once the war was over, he filed the first billion-dollar offering in the history of the SEC on behalf of Israel. Some might say the nice Jewish boy from Brooklyn did good—quite the mitzvah.

Don's constant travels to Israel had him working closely with Levi Eshkol who would become Israel's third Prime Minister, and subsequent finance ministers, including working closely with the Ministry of Defense.

Don remained active in his relationship with the State of Israel until 2013, and while he had taken a less driven position, until 2017 he represented the International Israel Bond Organization and was honored, in Israel, as a Founder of that organization.

The once 10-year-old kid who stood on a Brooklyn street corner, had made the international stage in the noblest of ways.

CHAPTER 8
PRACTICING LAW WITH THE GIANTS

"...Murray's biggest concern walking to the bench...was that he feared tripping over the long not yet hemmed robe..."
~ Don Bezahler

2018—Miami, FL

In January 2018, Don Bezahler's Miami doctors finally gave him the green light to travel. He flew to New York City with his wife Mary. They decided to catch a flick—"The Post"— and it brought back memories.

{Flashback —1962: Don Bezahler was hired by a high-powered and influential New York City law firm.}

"I joined one of the top firms in New York—Goldstein, Judd and Gurfein. The firm was prominent in both the legal world and in political circles. I was a young man on a mission," he remembered.

"As I sat and watched the film 'The Post', I reminisced how Murray Gurfein (portrayed in the flick) had been nominated by President Richard Nixon in 1971 to serve on the U.S. District Court for the Southern District of New York. Back in the day, it was tradition for the firm, which the newly minted judge had once served, to provide the robe the justice would wear. Unfortunately, our contribution was a bit on the long side. And since Murray hadn't had time to have it hemmed, he had to walk with great caution."

Justice Gurfein's first day on the bench found him doing nothing more cerebral than swearing in new citizens for nationalization.

{*Author's Note: In today's world this might not seem such a mundane exercise.*}

The following day, Gurfein was assigned to the "Pentagon Papers" case. Skeptical folk might infer that a Nixon appointee in the throes of such an imbroglio might be swayed. If so, the odds-makers were terribly off mark.

"Murray became quite the conversation piece when he refused the government's motion to keep the publication of the documents from going public. I visited Murray a few days after he'd heard the Pentagon case. He was dictating his opinion to his legal secretary. What I remember most," Don relayed with a laugh, "Was that Murray's biggest concern, walking to the bench on his second day on the court, was that he feared tripping over the long-hanging, not-yet-hemmed robe, and stumbling in front of the cameras!"

Speaking of illustrious partners, Orrin Grimmell Judd (another senior member), had another story altogether. In fact, he left the practice prior to Murray, and only with slightly less fanfare.

While Judd had served as Solicitor General of New York

State before joining the firm, in 1968 he was nominated by President Lyndon B. Johnson to a judgeship on the United States District Court for the Eastern District of New York.

Judd, like Gurfein, oversaw a ruling that would rock the foundation of American jurisprudence. During the first year of Nixon's initial term (1969), Nixon began bombings in Cambodia during the Vietnam War.

Don explained, "There was public outrage which segued into a lawsuit against the bombings and Judd caught the case. Nixon halted the aggression while the case was pending, but Judd ruled nonetheless (Holtzman v Schlesinger), and issued an injunction which prohibited the government from any military activities 'in or over Cambodia.' The case went all the way to the Supreme Court and was ultimately upheld!"

{*Author's Note: In an interesting twist, the departure of Judd found Don occupying the senior partner's office, Don having become a name partner in the firm.*}

As for Nathanial Goldstein, he'd already served as New York State Attorney General from 1943-1954 under the watch of Governor Thomas E. Dewey. He was most known for taking on the New York chapter of the Ku Klux Klan.

"Nathaniel was the man responsible for bringing me into the firm in the first place," Don said. "He had no further desires for public service and was comfortable in his hugely successful private practice. He stuck with the firm until his retirement."

CHAPTER 9
FROM CONDORS TO CABARET

"We wanted a big cash company. We knew that having a NYSE-listed company would be the launching pad for more and more acquisitions."
~ Don Bezahler

September 20, 2017—New York City—Rosh Hashanah

Don Bezahler was spending Shanah Tovah with long time family friends, the Goldmans (patriarch, Sol, and his brother, Irving—having long since passed). The connection, however, was established in the 1970's and has remained *mishpoches* (like extended family) ever since.

But it wasn't always so—not by a long shot. In fact, Sol and Don had a rather dicey introduction during their initial business dealings in the Naked City.

Thanks to some crafty manipulations by Don, the pair became and remained business associates with Don acting as Sol's attorney, helping Sol garner millions upon millions of dollars in myriad real estate maneuvers.

In fact, it was a *mea culpa* on the part of Sol that sealed their working relationship. "You're the only lawyer that ever beat me in anything. I want you to represent me in this mess," Sol said, in reference to the real estate crash of New York City during the early seventies which severely jeopardized his holdings.

So, at sundown on that special night in the City that Never Sleeps, Don (85-years-old) and the Goldman family celebrated the lighting of candles and a festive meal.

*****

In the late 1960's one of Don's biggest clients was Haven Industries, controlled by Donald Liederman and Neil Rosenstein. Haven was a public shell company *(according to Investopedia.com: A shell corporation is a corporation without active business operations or significant assets. Legitimate reasons for a shell corporation include such things as a startup using the business entity as a vehicle to raise funds, conduct a hostile takeover or to go public).*

Two of the corporation's initial endeavors (in which Don was very much involved) were the purchase of the Pittsburgh Condors (of the American Basketball Association) and the motion picture rights to the Broadway hit 'Cabaret.'

The Condor acquisition was calculated on more than rumor--it was widely understood that the NBA was going to absorb its fledgling competition, the ABA. It seemed like the fast track to the business of big-time professional basketball.

However, the Condors were bleeding money, and in a gamble, the Haven crew decided to sell the rights to Cabaret at a $36,000 profit, to feed the faltering hoopsters. Two years later, when the merger finally occurred, the NBA chose not to select the Pittsburgh Condors as an affiliate.

To Don's credit, the crafty Haven franchise, engaging in all type of promotions and off-beat sale shticks, arranged for an exhibition game against the Lew Alcindor-led Milwaukee Bucks, the first-ever game played between two teams from the separate organizations.

Despite this Bill Veeck type bravado, the Condors didn't cut it and the NBA took a pass.

"It was a disaster," said Don. "We bet on the wrong horse."

There is no doubt of that as in 1972 the film 'Cabaret,' directed by Bob Fosse, starring Liza Minnelli, and distributed by Allied, was a massive hit. Not only did the film score eight Oscars, but Don suffered the ignominy of sitting in his room at the Beverly Hills Hotel and having his wife Suzanne, who was attending the film's premiere at New York's Ziegfeld Theater, call him to say, "Did you made a mistake!" before hanging up.

{*Author's Note: To this day Don has never seen the movie.*}

Don and the Haven crew, however, were undaunted. What ensued was the company's biggest score—the takeover of NYSE hulk, National Sugar Refining Company, number two at the time, right behind Domino Sugar.

The path to this entitlement was no less treacherous than wading in the swamps of the ABA. Don said, "We found that one individual owned 33 percent of the company and so he was our natural target. He wouldn't sell, and we soon found out why—he'd committed to real-estate mogul Sol Goldman, and that was that—for the time being.

"We wanted a big cash company. We knew that having a NYSE-listed company would be the launching pad for more and more acquisitions." So, Don wrote to Sol, making an offer he couldn't possibly refuse—the promise of a $5 million dollar profit within two-weeks of the purchase.

Apparently, Don wasn't Don Corleone, and despite a handshake agreement, Sol terminated the deal before the ink was dry.

Determined, Don put together a package of securities (bonds, stocks and warrants). Factually, there was little, if any, value but there was the appearance of breath on the mirror held before the nose and mouth of a stiff.

Don did the old end-a-round and made an offer to the other 67 percent shareholders of the National Sugar Refining Company. The company he'd formed for such a feat was named YGAC (You Guys Are Crazy). As fate would have it, and in the hustle-and-bustle world of NYC biz, this bit of ballsy play paid off.

Sol and Don spoke again two-years later, and while the company was holding its own, let's just say the Haven crew was as needy as the Condors, and Don made an offer to Sol.

A deal was consummated. Sol became sole owner of National Sugar, but dang if that real estate bubble burst of the early 1970's didn't threaten to break the moorings of Sol's many Macy's Day Parade floats. You see, Sol's mortgages had become more substantial than the actual value of many of the properties.

And that's when the second handshake took place. Sol brought Don onboard as an attorney and advisor to straighten out his awful imbroglio and Don performed, ultimately unraveling the mess, and the road to prosperity was paved.

Shortly thereafter, Sol's sibling, Irving, also became a client and, well let's just say, the slot machine started in with a chorus of clang, clang, clang.

CHAPTER 10
BREAKING BREAD

"The ultimatum was met. The money was in the bank."
~ Don Bezahler

January 2018—Leopard des Artistes—New York City

Don Bezahler and his wife Mary were seated in the *très chic*, white tablecloth, art lavished, Upper West Side restaurant, Leopard des Artistes. Also seated at the table were two women Don has known since they were little girls, Dorian and Katja (*née* Goldman), and their husbands.

The Goldman relationship dates back to the early 1970's. It started with the gal's Uncle Sol and developed into a powerful bond between Don and their father Irving.

The nearly fifty-year friendship began as adversarial and wound up as one of advocacy. The Goldman "account" was Don's longest running and most lucrative—and this despite the fact that it took a bit of skullduggery on Don's part to win Sol over in the first place.

In any event, the six-top sat sipping fine champagne and dining on the cuisine of Northern Italy. Don, every bit the father figure, remained a trusted advisor of the family's real estate empire.

*****

In a previous chapter you read about Don's introduction to the Goldman family and its vast financial interests, when Don and Sol Goldman engaged in a game of *tete-a-tete*, with a dash of bravado from each side.

Don's crew, Haven Industries, wanted respectability by owning a NYSE company. At the time, Horace Havemeyer owned a 33 percent share of National Sugar Refining Company.

Representing Haven Industries, Don made an offer. Horace turned him down, and a few weeks later Don learned via the media that Horace had sold his shares to real estate magnate, Sol Goldman, and his partner, Alex DiLorenzo.

{Author's Note: To put the enormity of the Goldman/DiLorenzo holdings in perspective, consider this quote from the New York Times in 1975: "Alex DiLorenzo Jr., who with his partner, Sol Goldman, built and operated the largest real estate empire in New York City..."}

If anything, this turn of events inspired the indefatigable Don, and so he switched tactics and set his sights on Goldman, making a bold offer, "Sell your shares for cost within the next two weeks and we'll guarantee a $5 million bonus."

Needless to say, Sol was all ears but demanded evidence of the solubility of Don's group. He required the money be transferred to a Haven account at Chase Manhattan Bank as proof of their ability to consummate the deal.

The ultimatum was met and "the money was in the bank" but then Sol flipped the script.

"When I met with Sol, he wanted to negotiate the asking

price. I advised that the price was firm—take it or leave it. Sol left the deal on the table," Don said, adding, "If you can't get to the minority owner, you go for the majority."

And that's just what he did. Eventually, Don and Haven purchased the 70 percent shares, and suddenly Sol's position and holdings were marginalized. Then, prior to the real estate collapse in New York City, the Haven group needed some liquidity, and in an ironic twist, Don managed to sell Sol the 70 percent shares owned by their group.

DiLorenzo, in Donald Trump style, had one last parting shot (he died shortly thereafter). He called Don into his office and said, "I've been waiting to say this to you for years. You're fired!"

In the mid-1970's, the New York City real estate boom bottomed out and Sol Goldman was in trouble. Who did he turn to? Why Don, of course, the one guy who had beaten him at his own game.

"It was during this period that I first met Sol's brother, Irving. Irving and I clicked, and a friendship and business relationship ensued. It was then that I became close to Irving's children, son Lloyd and daughters Dorian and Katja."

Despite the dire environment, Don managed to preserve a substantial portion of Sol's assets. Once Don had the Goldman brother's stabilized, DiLorenzo's son went for the kill. A turf battle over property and proprietorship ensued. Don, representing the Goldmans, buried the DiLorenzo scion.

In sharing the story, Don commented, "Perhaps the moral

to this cautionary tale is that you simply never know where, or how, friendships and continued business relationships may be fostered. In the case of the Goldman family, our relationship started as a chess match. Respect was the end game—a long standing business and personal relationship, the overall outcome."

CHAPTER 11
FALSE IMPRESSIONS

*"I stepped inside to find comedian Buddy Hackett seated on
the couch…watching himself on the television."*
~ Don Bezahler

December 1965—Acapulco Bay, Mexico

Don and Suzanne were on their honeymoon, the impulsive
couple having recently tied the knot.

Under a cloudy sky Don walked the shoreline while
Suzanne participated in her favorite afternoon ritual of poker
and tequila with her new acquaintances in the lobby of the
Posada del Sol hotel.

Don spotted what seemed to be a swimmer in distress.
There is no one else on the beach. When he heard the pleas,
he knew he had no choice—Don shed his shoes and went into
the drink.

*****

Don and his first wife Norma were divorced in 1962.
Through the ensuing years of resumed bachelorhood, Don
dated frequently but had no steady—no one in particular. That
all changed in the fall of 1964.

"I'd been invited to a party on Park Avenue and 72nd

Street. Unfortunately, I'd invited a gal friend from Washington to visit on the very same day, and so I couldn't fully commit."

Don ultimately did attend the soiree—his plan was to stick around for a while and then head over to pick up his visiting date at her hotel.

"I was on the terrace chatting up a gal; her name was Teri Linde. Suddenly my eyes locked upon a stunner. I guess Teri noticed me noticing. But far from being insulted, she informed me the girl I was ogling was actually her best friend. Further, she asked if I'd like to be introduced!"

In short order Teri brought her friend out to the terrace, made the introductions and sort of slipped away. "I was enchanted, and as we spoke and laughed and drank, I fairly well forgot about my previous commitment. Eventually, I came to my senses and called my date at her hotel and suggested she meet me at the party."

Less than thrilled, the Washington gal soon arrived, quickly tired, and left while Don wound up spending the evening with Suzanne and ultimately escorting her home.

{*Author's Note: While Don could not recall the name of the Washington woman, he clearly recalled Suzanne's address: 211 E. 53rd Street.*}

"We were standing in the hallway, just outside her apartment door—wrapping things up, exchanging numbers, etc. when a voice from inside boomed, 'You're making too much noise. I'm watching myself on television!'"

Suzanne invited Don inside.

"I stepped inside to find comedian Buddy Hackett seated on the couch, indeed watching himself on the television. That was something. We schmoozed for a while before I bid Suzanne goodbye," he said with a grin.

{Author's Note: Suzanne lived with three other roommates— all female—one of whom was Hackett's opening act, singer Judy Scott.}

At this period of his life and career, Don was frequently traveling, and he left on one such junket the following day.

"I was away from town for four days and when I returned, I immediately called Suzanne. She was shocked that I hadn't kept in touch. She informed me that I was the only gentleman she'd met at the party who hadn't. Well, that was that. We began dating seriously—I suppose you could say I began courting," he recalled.

Don was in Phoenix, Arizona on business in November 1965, when "*The*" question was popped, only he wasn't the one who popped it!

"I had a client in the office when my phone rang, and Suzanne was on the other end. She asked what I was doing on December 2nd. I advised her that I was free that day. 'Then let's get married,' was her response! My stunned demeanor was not lost on the client who inquired as to the problem just as soon as I'd hung up the receiver. 'I think I'm getting married on December 2nd,' I told him. 'You're invited, and I want you to be my best man.'"

Word of Don's pending nuptials quickly spread throughout

the office and the deal was sealed. "We decided on a small wedding with immediate family only. We would be married in New York's Temple Emanu-El."

Following the ceremony, the party headed over to the Colony Restaurant before hosting a rousing gala at the Essex House attended by at least 100 family members, friends and associates.

{*Author's Note: The Colony played host to a who's who of actors, authors, artists, politico's and high-society. It was also the first restaurant in the U.S. to serve Dom Pérignon.*}

"I had a previously-scheduled business trip to Puerto Rico slated only days after our wedding, and so we took something of a pre-honeymoon jaunt to the island. While we were there, we decided that we ought to honeymoon, officially, in Mexico, sometime around Christmas," he shared.

"You have to understand, I had many powerful contacts in Mexico City due to the fact that I traveled there, on business, monthly. I felt we'd be treated as royalty, and Suzanne would be greatly impressed."

What Don hadn't factored in was attempting to get accommodations in Acapulco at the last minute, during the Christmas season, was nothing short of impossible.

"We arrived in Mexico City and had no problem securing a room in my usual hotel. However, when I tried my luck in Acapulco I was shut down! In a bit of a panic, and certainly in a pinch, I quickly called my key contact in Mexico and explained my dilemma. He rode to the rescue. Apparently, he owned a quaint but classy boutique hotel in Acapulco and while he too was fully booked, he cancelled an existing reservation and got us our honeymoon suite!"

It was a blissful and stress free time for the newlyweds. They dined and swam and shopped and romanced—that is, until one fateful day.

"It was cloudy, probably the only poor weather day of our stay. Susanne was indulging in her new favorite afternoon pastime—poker and tequila with a crew she'd befriended," Don recalled.

"Anyway, I decided to walk the shore of Acapulco Bay. I was strolling along when I saw what I believed to be a swimmer in distress. Once he began screaming for help, it was obvious. I looked around but there was absolutely no one else nearby. I knew what must be done and I swam out to the struggling swimmer."

"There's a reason the professionals urge you not to just jump in. That's because a panicked drowning victim will struggle to use the saver as a foothold and typically both wind up at the bottom of the sea. And that's exactly what happened. This guy freaked out and I had to fight mightily to not only save him, but to save myself!"

"I guess the drama caught the attention of the hotel staff and while I was prone and panting on shore in the sand, a concerned Suzanne stood over me. Then the other guy's wife showed up—a regular family affair."

"Now, I'll be honest, while I had no ulterior motives in

saving the guy in the first place, my mind did begin to conjure scenarios. Perhaps I'd saved a billionaire who would be forever in my debt. Such thoughts swirled and I actually invited the guy and his wife to dinner that evening."

"As it turns out, this fella wasn't rich or particularly keen on thanking me at all. Apparently, he was a regular Joe, dying of a brain tumor. The near drowning was actually a suicide attempt, but he had second thoughts. So here I'm picking up the tab for a guy who feels badly about his cowardice, but nothing for me. In fact, his wife seemed equally perturbed by his lack of spine. And here I almost lost my life!"

Perhaps that event was portent of what would eventually befall Don's marriage to Suzanne.

CHAPTER 12
A NEW ROLE

The next day, while nursing a hangover, Don is advised that he was making a meatball and spaghetti supper for eight.

1979—Offices of Goldstein, Judd & Gurfein—Madison Avenue, New York City

Don Bezahler had been carrying on a relationship with his secretary for almost a decade. Apparently, the end game was significantly different in the view of the two. While Don had no serious intentions, his secretary was hell-bent on a husband by the time her clock ticked to thirty-years of age.

As a result of this discrepancy of perspective, the secretary told Don, flat-out, that if he didn't leave his wife and commit to her, she would kill him. He did not believe her, but the death ultimatum was the second delivered to the barrister in that very same office, over a ten-year span...

*****

THE RING

Don had purchased a modest 2.2 carat engagement ring for Suzanne. One she seemed to wear proudly.

Only days after the honeymoon ended and the couple were ensconced once again in Don's one-bedroom apartment at 1175 York Avenue in Manhattan, Don had to leave for Israel on business. Since Suzanne was working at the time, the trip was a solo excursion.

"While I was in Israel, I purchased some not-very-expensive rings and assorted jewelry for Suzanne Nothing that broke the bank—trinkets really. When I returned bearing the gifts, Suzanne decided to wear those rings rather than her engagement ring."

Sometime later, the apartment was burglarized and the wedding and engagement rings were among the stolen loot. Don didn't replace it, but Suzanne sure did!

"Among Suzanne's proclivities was bidding at Christie's Auction House," Don said. "She came home with a 16.5 carat ring, proclaiming that it so much resembled her engagement ring. Perhaps on steroids, I thought. But I paid for it. She told me she would cherish it forever."

{Author's Note: Years later, shortly after their divorce, Don noticed an auction advertised in the Miami Herald. Among the goodies up for grabs—Suzanne's precious ring.}

THE APARTMENT & A PAD IN THE HAMPTONS

"Suzanne felt that the robbery was an inside job, perhaps involving the doorman or another employee of the building. In any event, she became paranoid and the only option was to move," Don said, thinking back to those days.

"As it happened, a client of our law firm owned an apartment building at 923 5th Avenue—a tony address and an enviable building. In 1969 we moved in, and we stayed for the next 15 years."

Don was working hard and making good money which Suzanne was fond of spending. "I enjoyed the finer things in life and worked tirelessly to afford them, but with Suzanne it was almost an obsession."

In the early 1970's, the Hampton's were coming into their own—the place to be for Manhattanites who could afford the luxury of an end-of-the-island getaway.

Don and Suzanne purchased a modest home in West Hampton Beach. "On one particular trip to the island, I found a contractor building a house next to the one owned by a client. It was a spec project, meaning there was no buyer or owner at the time. In any event, I began putting in my two cents, suggesting all types of modifications to his plans. Oddly, he adapted them all."

"Once the house was complete the builder says to me 'We never discussed price!' Frankly, I hadn't been interested beyond my continued kvetching, but negotiations began and I purchased the house, adding a swimming pool, tennis court, and strolling gardens. This became our weekend getaway. Suzanne was, of course, quite pleased."

"One weekend, right after the tennis court had been

completed, I was standing, gazing at my 'Castle', proud of the fact that some poor guy from Brooklyn had addresses on both 5th Avenue and the Hamptons."

Don was jolted from his reverie by some guy standing beside him asking if he'd like to play a set of tennis on his brand-new court. And who should it be making yet another cameo in the movie of Don's life but comedian Buddy Hackett.

MEATBALLS AND JAGUARS

Fortunately, Don Bezahler wasn't in a courtroom (instead a cocktail party) when he offered to prepare his famous spaghetti and meatballs. Rather than a violation of Judicial Conduct, it was just a little white lie mixed up in a whole lot of red sauce.

"Suzanne and I had a group of friends, we were four couples in all, who frequently dined together. In fact, it was almost a Saturday ritual. We'd eat at one restaurant or another throughout the week, except on Saturdays when the Hampton's were so busy it was next to impossible to get a table – especially for eight."

"So, we created something of a supper club. Each couple would take a turn hosting the others for a home-cooked meal on Saturday nights. It was a Friday evening, the eve before it was our turn to play hosts, when, while a bit imbibed, I pronounced that I would be preparing my famous spaghetti and meatballs the following evening."

"The next day, while nursing a hang-over, Suzanne advised me that I was making a meatball spaghetti supper for eight that very evening!"

And while Don accepted Suzanne's version of the night before, and his blustery boast, the fact of the matter was, Don couldn't cook, and especially not meatballs, let alone "famous" meatballs with marinara sauce.

Undaunted, the Dragon Slayer began calling all the local Italian eateries.

"The problem was none of these places would provide me the twenty meatballs and sauce I needed (I was counting on Suzanne to cook the pasta so the entire meal would feel freshly made). These establishments would only consider eight separate entrees. I wouldn't have it!"

Don finally found a sympathetic restaurant and arranged a pickup for that afternoon. Sensing he'd scored his coup, when the appointed time came, Don hopped into the brand new Jaguar convertible he'd recently purchased for his wife.

"The whole kit-and-caboodle came in a huge tin, which I had the staff place into the trunk of the Jag," he said. "I was nearing home when I hit a bump in the road. I could hear the pan bouncing around.

When I pulled in, I opened the trunk only to find sauce everywhere – fortunately the meatballs had stayed put. In any event, under the scornful watch of Suzanne, I spent the next hour or so cleaning the boot of the Jag."

By 6:30 that evening the guests began arriving. Don had put the meatballs and remaining sauce in a huge pot – he was wearing an apron, standing over the stove, stirring the concoction, his game face unshakable.

"My friends marveled at the sight and aromas. They couldn't believe I could actually cook. When they asked how long I'd been at it, I replied 'Since 2 p.m.!'"

The wine and champagne began to pour liberally and by 8 p.m. Don was ready to break out the goodies. "To a person, they savored my meatballs and sauce and when they began to plead for my recipe, I felt forced to announce it was a long-held secret, one which I was unwilling to reveal, even to such close friends."

"I suspect by that point Suzanne had heard enough. She spilled the beans, in the process busting my meat-balls!"

A good laugh was had by all, but from that point on, Don gave up cooking and Suzanne took the reins of all further fine cuisine obligations.

THE FIRE

In the late 1970's Don and Suzanne's summer home in West Hampton Beach had become more of a year 'round place for Suzanne, who was fond of the Island and her independence. Meanwhile, Don hunkered down in their opulent Manhattan apartment during the week while working at the law firm.

In any event, it was a typical weekday. Don was at

the office when word came of a massive fire raging on Long Island, and it was heading towards their exclusive enclave.

"I knew Suzanne would be in a panic, especially after the fire jumped the main roadway heading for our house." Don knew what he must do--rescue Suzanne and the house, if possible. The logistical problem was that the Long Island Expressway was shut down as a result of the blaze.

"I got in my car, broke out my map, and found an alternative route. I had to drive north rather than east in order to sweep around the fire." Don kept his eye on the road and the map, his ears tuned intently to the steady news reports coming over the radio.

After three hours of driving, Don had made it to the other side of the inferno, but it was still far east of where he needed to be.

"I found back roads which placed me within three or four miles of our home. I could actually see the flames crossing the main Hampton artery, NY 27. It took another hour to get to the house!"

With flames a mere ten-blocks from Suzanne and their home, Don arrived. "Suzanne was a wreck, everyone who had actually been in the neighborhood seemed to have already evacuated, and since it was off-season, many of the manses were empty of occupants anyways."

"Suzanne couldn't believe that I'd made it. She was never so happy to see me. I knew we had to beat a hasty retreat, so we piled into the car and kept driving east. We eventually came upon a motel, far from the reach of the fire, and checked in."

The following day found the fire under control, which allowed for Don and Suzanne to return to their property to assess the damage. "It was amazing. The scorched landscape--the trees on the corner where we lived were blackened and burnt to a crisp. The house, however, was untouched. Apparently, the winds changed, moving the flames in a different direction, roughly 100 yards from our property!"

And while Don had experienced being under fire during his Army stint in Austria –this was a fire he'd dodged by rushing towards the fight rather than seeking cover.

FATAL ATTRACTION

{*Author's Note: While Suzanne may have been preoccupied by materialism, Don had more carnal tastes, and was carrying on an affair with his law firm's secretary.*}

"There was a meeting at the office attended by some of our team, including myself, the client, and a few other people he'd brought with him. There was one woman in particular, who was unknown to me, but who did participate in the sit-down," Don shared.

"The following day, my secretary came into my office. She was always welcome of course, but she seemed a bit rattled. She explained that the woman from the previous day was outside, demanding that she meet with me. My secretary had thought it out--I'd meet with this woman and after fifteen minutes she would interrupt, reminding me that I had another appointment."

"When the visitor entered my office, she had a strange look in her eyes, almost a feral continence, nothing resembling the person from the day before. When she spoke, it only got worse. 'I had a dream last night,' she told me. 'I was in the park and you were on an island in the park. And I started swimming out to you. I need you to make love to me. You must, otherwise I'm going to kill you!'"

Don's response was to laugh, but he realized this woman was both serious and potentially psychotic. Fortunately, as per the script, the secretary ushered the panting paramour out of the office.

"I immediately called the client from the initial meeting, and while we couldn't be too direct, due to ethical protocol, she did provide me with the name of a psychiatrist who confirmed that the person in question had issues."

"Concerned, I called the police, but they could do nothing unless she did something more substantial. At that point, I quit walking to work and hired a car service instead. I was genuinely concerned for my safety."

Of course, Don explained the situation to Suzanne. But her reaction was to accuse Don of having an affair with this woman. "Suzanne was pissed. She truly thought I was involved with this wackadoo. That is, until the subject called our private number and Suzanne had the opportunity to listen in. At that point her anger turned to fear. Fortunately, shortly thereafter I was advised by the psychiatrist that the woman had been committed—the drama was over."

Or so Don thought. A few years later his secretary and sometime lover, utterly frustrated by the status quo, apparently believed Don would leave Suzanne and marry her.

She asked, hadn't Don and Suzanne grown apart? Hadn't Don explained that he and Suzanne resembled friends more than husband and wife? Wasn't their marriage for all practical purposes a fraud?

The secretary threatened to kill Don if he didn't leave Susanne and marry her. She was quickly and quietly transferred to the Florida offices of the firm.

CHAPTER 13
LIFE WITH MARY BEGINS

"I was heading for the door of the conference room when I noticed a beautiful young woman exiting the elevator, headed in my direction."
~ Don Bezahler

2010—The Tower House, Miami Beach, FL

After 44-years Don Bezahler's marriage was over. Kaput!

Don was driving his Mercedes Benz north on A-1-A, leaving his wife and headed toward the love of his life.

"I was single for thirty-minutes," Don said with nary a hint of lament.

*****

In 2004, Don was splitting his time between Miami Beach and New York City. Don's business in Florida was Preferred Employers Holdings Inc., and his associate was Mel Harris.

Preferred Employers Holdings was established to buy failing or wounded companies, turn them around, and then sell them to the highest bidder (a well-crafted and most successful endeavor).

One day, Mel pulled Don aside. He mentioned how a

mutual friend had suggested the duo meet with a woman who was seeking investors for her fledgling company.

"It was February," Don said matter-of-factly, recalling the month of an event that happened thirteen-years ago. "To be frank, our company did not invest, that wasn't our model. However, since we both had respect for the contact, we decided, as a courtesy, to meet with this entrepreneur."

The meeting was set to take place in the conference room at the offices of Preferred Employers Holdings. "I was heading for the door of the conference room when I noticed a beautiful young woman exiting the elevator and head in my direction. I admit, from the moment I set my eyes upon Mary I was smitten—initially struck by her beauty."

While Mary's presentation was impressive and duly noted by both partners, they, nonetheless, decided to take a pass. Don took it upon himself to be the bearer of bad news.

In a phone call Don explained, apologetically, that while Mary was professional and convincing, Preferred Employers Holdings simply didn't invest in start-up companies.

Perhaps sleeping dogs lie, but not Mary Mathis! A few weeks after Don's doomsday call, Mary called him back. She explained she had an opportunity to bring some staff to New York to meet with a major firm. Seeking mentorship beforehand, she asked Don if they might get together to discuss it.

And meet up they did, at the Gourmet Diner on Biscayne Boulevard in Miami Beach. Sadly, a third-wheel scenario ensued as Mary showed up with the very same woman who had introduced her to the company in the first place.

Over the breaking of bread, Mary described what she had hoped to accomplish on this business venture. That said, she was also a little slim in the funding department. Mary reckoned that it would take $2,500 to make the jaunt a reality.

Don, without pause, reached into his breast pocket, pulled out a personal check, penned the digits and signed. When Mary returned from New York she called Don, relaying the results of the trip. Mary invited Don to her office on Moffett Street in Hollywood to further the discussion.

Don accepted.

During that meeting, Mary, after being debriefed on the New York excursion, asked Don if he'd consider making a personal investment in her company—something outside Preferred Employers Holdings' purview.

Needless to say, Don had to sleep on it, and a follow up "dinner-date" at Fulvios was suggested. "It was odd. When I pulled up to Mary's place to pick her up, that gal, the one who'd brought Mary to the table in the first place, was there— again. Which frankly was fine, as this was, after all, business. It became a bit awkward when our company excused herself to use the powder room, and Mary asked if I'd invited her to join us."

The pair managed to lose the potential "snake-in-the-grass" and met a few more times sans the 3rd wheel.

Eventually, a deal for $300,000 was struck. The qualifier,

however, was that Mary would report to Don daily. He wanted to know how the money was being spent and the results thereof.

Certainly, the story up to this point is leading to a sordid romance novel scenario. After all, both Don and Mary had significant others at the time. However, the itch, perhaps imprisoned just below the surface, was kept on ice as the relationship, to this point, remained purely professional.

Don and Mary's platonic intimacy drew them closer. Soon the daily calls became speckled with dinners and lunches. And after ten months of this on-going relationship, Don invited Mary to join him in New York where they would stay at the Carlyle Hotel.

And while Don saw to it that their suite was appointed for romance—dozens of roses and champagne on ice, he nonetheless kept his carnal cravings in check. At least long enough to close a $300 million deal on his cell phone in a stairwell at the Carlyle while Mary remained bemused at the front desk, waiting to check in.

The affair carried on for months and months but both lovers knew they couldn't continue with such subterfuge. They agreed they would divorce their spouses. Mary was the first to take the plunge.

"I remember Mary saying to me, 'Well I got divorced, how about you?'" Don wasn't shirking. After all, dissolving a forty-four-year marriage can be complicated, but Don and Suzanne managed to come to an agreement.

As a "parting gift," Suzanne expressed to Don her strong desire to be honored at the Love and Hope Ball in Miami. Stars such as Bee Gees' Barry Gibbs was active with the charity and would attend and perform.

Not only did Don make a very generous contribution, he also purchased two-tables, inviting twenty friends and family. To Don's surprise both he and his wife were honored, a nice flourish to the end of a long chapter in his life.

The following February, Don was once again in his Mercedes Benz, heading north from Miami Beach to Hollywood—to the Hollywood home of the woman he would eventually marry.

"As I was driving towards Mary, I thought to myself, 'What a start to a weird adventure.' Frankly, I suspected I'd move in with Mary as was proposed, but keep the condo after Suzanne moved out. I'd split my time between the two residences."

Or so he thought. You see, Don and Mary became inseparable.

"Any thoughts of a duel existence were soon dashed. I was crazy for Mary. I recall my friends being dazzled that I could live in a modest home in Hollywood. Frankly, I couldn't believe it myself. I'd never lived in a house in my entire adult life—doorman buildings, plush, massive-square-foot condos were more my style."

While Mary and Don often frequented local restaurants and attended any number of social events, they always spent New Year's Eve at home—indulging on the finest caviar, the best champagne, and selected music to imbibe by.

And then, on one such New Year's Eve, Mary suggested marriage. Don heartily agreed. The proverb "Home is where the heart is" is attributed to Roman philosopher Pliny the Elder, and Don's heart was clearly with Mary.

The couple continued, until 2019, residing in that home by the beach that they refurbished together, in the humble hamlet of Hollywood.

Love trumps all.

CHAPTER 14
TRIALS AND TRIBULATIONS OF A LONG MARRIAGE

"I always thought we were on the same page. We had a game plan, each of our roles clearly defined."
~ Don Bezahler

1973—Central Park Zoo, New York City

Don Bezahler went on his typical morning stroll. One which took him from his posh 5th Avenue apartment, through Central Park, with a stop at the zoo, before heading off to his office at 60th and Madison Avenue.

One morning Don realized he was spending more time with the Central Park polar bears than with his wife, Suzanne.

"When I first met Suzanne, I was smitten. Suzanne was attractive, articulate and had social skills. Frankly, I thought she'd be good for my career, an asset."

Both Suzanne and Don were on the same page—in the beginning. Don was throwing himself—headlong—into building a career and making a fortune for his fledgling family.

"I never really paid attention to the early red-flags. I was fully committed to my career and working tirelessly. Poor Suzanne would take cooking classes and I was never home for dinner. Instead, I'd have her meet me at some restaurant—her culinary efforts gone to waste."

The couple essentially became strangers under the same roof. Don would be up early and off to the office while Suzanne was still in bed. He'd return in evening, typically around 8:30 p.m.

"I don't recall us every having breakfast or lunch together," he said.

It was business, business, business—even their social circle was comprised of associates, clients, and partners. "One time, Suzanne lamented that it would be nice to go out with a cop or a fireman—something, anything, different than the status quo."

But that wasn't about to happen. Don was typically working 13-hour days. During the first three years of the marriage he never took a single day off, and while they were able to afford a luxury home in the Hamptons (their weekend getaway), Don brought business with him.

"I'd have documents delivered on Saturday, pore over them, and send them back on Sunday so I wouldn't miss a beat on Monday. I was driven, and perhaps this drove Suzanne a bit batty. To a certain extent I regret never truly taking Suzanne's feelings or desires into consideration. I always thought we were on the same page. We had a game plan, each of our roles clearly defined. I was building an empire for the both of us, or so I thought."

And then there was David, Don's young son from his first marriage. David would often spend time with the couple in the Hamptons on weekends—this created a further chasm in the intimacy department.

"On hindsight, I realize that Suzanne wasn't cut out for the 'role' she'd been selected. She wasn't thrilled at playing hostess—she was shy, not snooty. Quite frankly, it wasn't a good fit for her. Plus, I wanted another child—she didn't. Her life became more a chore than a joy."

After a decade of demur deception; Don and Suzanne sunk into the routine of roommates—perhaps friends, but certainly not husband and wife. Nonetheless, from the outside, the couple appeared to have everything—an enviable existence, but it was a facade.

"I began coming home later and later—working even more hours. And that's the type of denial we'd both embraced. The perception of the 'good life' had us fooled."

Once Don purchased a condo in Miami Beach, where Suzanne spent more and more of her time alone, even friends and associates began to get the picture. Far from idyllic, the relationship was listing gravely.

"The Miami condo was actually a real blessing. We were already, spiritually and emotionally, living apart. Now we could do it physically. I felt free for the first time in a long time," Don admitted.

What ensued was a move to a grander scale apartment

on East 54th Street, the sale of the Hamptons digs, and then the purchase of another. They tried travel but dulled on it. After 44 years of marriage, the writing was on the wall.

In a last-ditch effort to salvage the marriage, Suzanne offered up a proposition. If Don were to give up Mary, she would agree to reconciliation and make a go of it.

"Ironically, at the same time, Mary had drawn her own line in the sand. She said, 'I'm not going to be your Tuesday and Friday girl any longer!'"

Don had a choice—his options clear. Without pause, he chose a life with Mary. The pair is still happily married!

CHAPTER 15
A SPRING BLOOM IN AUTUMN

"I had no hobbies, no quick available distractions. I'd worked my entire adult life...grooming my legal career."
~ Don Bezahler

2003—New York City

It was a spring bloom in autumn, a period of semi-retirement, introspection, and puppy-love developing into a full-blown bark.

"In 2003, I decided to reduce my workload for a number of reasons. As a senior partner in our law firm, I was the only one resisting a possible merger with another large legal firm. But perhaps more importantly, a bit of a malaise was setting in. Honestly, when you've hit the top of the legal profession, where do you go from there," Don asked.

The fact was, Don was 71 years old at the time, and perhaps beyond being bored, he was a bit fatigued. After all, seventy-hour workweeks can wear on even a spring chicken.

"It was only natural that I began handing off the 'trench' work to the younger staff members—a crew whom I had mentored. I decided to approach my two biggest clients (one in New York, the other in Miami), and offer up a new working relationship. I would become president and chief operating officer of Preferred Employers Holdings in Miami and a consultant to the Goldman family, both entailing far less day-in-and-day-out involvements. The proposed remuneration was substantial. I would spend one week in Miami, the next in New York, and then repeat the cycle."

This allowed Don a partial retirement package. He would put in the time and effort and supervise his underlings in their due diligence.

The clients signed on.

Don loved the travel and especially the newly found freedom from the drudgery of insane hours of work.

Ahh, but the proverbial fly in the ointment! You see, while Don had more free time on his hands, he hadn't an inkling of what to do with it.

"I had no hobbies, no quick, available distractions. I'd worked my entire adult life tirelessly grooming my legal career, and then I met Mary."

Suddenly, the vacuum was filled. "With Mary, I found myself doing things I'd never done with Norma or Suzanne. It's odd, but in a few short months I had a deeper, more intimate relationship with Mary than I'd had with either of my wives, and that was without the additional benefit of sex."

"You see, suddenly, I was *sharing* time with someone. Mary and I would visit the Vizcaya Museum and Gardens in Miami, we'd attend lectures, have lunches, discuss things I'd found mundane before. Mary was a God-send, a breath of fresh air."

Don suddenly found himself the embodiment of the John Lennon song "Watching the Wheels." He just had to let it go, and while still much involved in his career, the phone no longer rang at 8 a.m. He was no longer on the treadmill, but rather on a straightaway to love and happiness.

"Coffee in the morning replaced putting on a suit. Instead of taking thirty business-related calls a day, I'd speak with Mary ten times a day," he said, smiling.

Don and Mary had started as strangers, became like-minded amoebae, then business partners, and eventually friends until, finally, love blossomed.

"With time on my hands, I embraced intimacy for the first time. This was an emotion I'd abandoned in pursuit of my smashing and successful career. It most certainly wasn't the fault of Norma or Suzanne and especially not my son, David. We'd all bought into the scenario, at some level, and I had run with it."

"But now, introspection was given a toe-hold. The 'What's It All About' quandary, the mellowness of aged wine, these were suddenly the questions and answers that defined the autumn of my life. Rather than a great lawyer from New York, I became a better human-being in Florida."

{*Author's Note: Don and Mary married and remain happily ensconced in a loving, explorative relationship. Don's involvement with his son, David, has been redefined in full-fledged filial affection. Asia, the Golden Retriever, tugs at her leash as the love-*

birds follow, making their way down the Boardwalk and into the golden years of Don Bezahler's life.}

MARY AND DON

February 2010 – The Love and Hope Ball is over, and Don moves from 5500 Collins Avenue in Miami Beach into 320 Polk Street, Hollywood, Florida, 30 minutes away by car.

Don had mixed feelings--5500 had good memories. He had been president of the Condo Association for many years and had solved problems arising from a $1 million theft from the Association. The building was the second most prestigious in Miami Beach and Don left a beautiful 3,000 square foot apartment.

320 Polk Street was another story. The landscape consisted of mud and sand and the house, although 50 feet from the sand and ocean, was in pretty bad condition and needed almost a total renovation. Mary and a girlfriend had moved there in 1999, and Mary had lived there with her second husband. To say the least, Don was not exactly ecstatic.

However, Mary and Don had a great relationship, were very much in love, and nothing could keep them apart. Don's office in Miami was 40 minutes away, while it was 15-20 minutes from the apartment in Miami Beach.

To make things more challenging, Don had never lived in a house, having lived in apartments all his life. Sure, he had houses in the Hamptons, but these were for weekends, not daily living.

Undaunted, Mary and Don decided to make Polk Street the home where they could spend the rest of their lives together. With a positive attitude (mostly), they embarked on a three-year adventure to re-do the house. Mary bore the brunt of the task, since Don would spend most of his time in the Miami office or New York City.

No amount of hardship could interfere with their idyllic life. Obviously they ate out a lot, but spent their time together in love and harmony. They travelled to see Don's son and his wife, to Israel, to Paris, to Australia, and to Bali as well as Vermont for summer weekends. And there was a memorable trip to London, Cannes and Monte Carlo. As Mary used to say, "War is Hell!"

After three long years and tons of money, the house was completed. Mary had turned it into a beautiful home with magnificent gardens all around the house. Shangri La was completed.

"MARY AND DON" MARRIAGE

December 31, 2011 – New Year's Eve – Mary and Don had decided to tie the knot. Because each had been married and divorced twice before, they thought only a small wedding was warranted.

The couple agreed that their nuptials ought to be a quiet, private affair, with immediate family only. However, once word got out among their circle of friends, a particularly ornery member of the crew protested vehemently.

"'You're not cheating me out of a wedding, Don Bezahler!' Those were her words." Don chuckled.

The ultimate decision was finalized by something of a cosmic happenstance. While Mary and Don were strolling New York City, arm in arm, they came upon The Community Church of New York (40 East 35th Street).

Mary was suddenly startled. Her eyes fixed upon signage in front of this place of worship. She pointed to the name Reverend Bruce Southworth.

"Reverend Southworth was the minister at the church in Roanoke, Virginia, when I was enrolled at Hollins University!" she exclaimed.

The duo soon attended a service, confirming Reverend Southworth was indeed the minister from Roanoke. "We approached Southworth after the service. Mary introduced herself, revealing their Virginia-Hollins connection," Don recalled. "We asked if he'd perform our wedding ceremony. His initial reaction was reticence. He brought up our age difference and my religious leanings, or lack thereof, as his core concerns. But after a few hours of conversation he accepted our request."

The "guest list" was tidy, some thirty-plus close friends and family, including the lady from Florida who had demanded a public ceremony in the first place.

"My son, David, served as best man, while his wife Amber

was Mary's matron of honor. Gerald A. Brown, a noted music director at the New York City Opera and rehearsal pianist under Leonard Bernstein at the New York Philharmonic, directed the music. Famed florist, Maria Christina Niño, added her floral touches. It was quite an affair."

Mary and Don scripted the ceremony, wrote their own vows, and the wedding went off without a hitch, other than them being hitched.

After the wedding, the party loaded into limousines and headed to the vaunted '21' Club. It was a picture-perfect ending to a gloriously stunning wedding—but it wasn't over. Not by a long shot.

"Our friends in Florida were pissed off! I suspect they'd felt slighted," Don said. So, what did Mary and Don do? Why, they hosted another reception for said friends and associates at Aqualina, the 5-Star resort in Sunny Isles.

"There had to be at least a hundred people present. It was an over-the-top extravaganza. The booze flowed and the celebration lasted until the wee hours."

*****

It was beautiful from the start and it continues to this day. Each of their lives has blossomed, and each day brings new and deeper bonds between them. Don has decided to live to 100, and Mary thinks that is not enough.

Miracles do happen, and Don considers his relationship with Mary to be a miracle. It took a lot for them to get together, and they each believe the miracle will last forever.

CHAPTER 16
GOING UNDER THE KNIFE

"Is there a doctor on board?" Three showed up.

October 21st, 2017—Hollywood, FL

"My doctors told me that without the surgery I'd have no more than two years to live, but that I might drop dead at any time," Don stated matter-of-factly of his upcoming open-heart surgery, while his loyal, four-legged friend, Asia (pronounced Ah-See-Ah) scampered about, nuzzling her master.

"To be honest, if it were not for Mary—the woman I love so dearly—I would pass on the operation. Look, I've had a full and wonderful life. I've done it all. However, Mary still needs me, and I feel that I have more to do in preparation for her, before I pass. And so, I'm going under the knife."

"And let me tell you the ultimate irony," Don said, a broad smile upon his face. "My aortic valve might be replaced with one from a pig. What do you know, a non-kosher body-part in a nice Jewish boy from Brooklyn."

We laughed out loud despite knowing, full-well, this was no average open-heart surgery—not by a long shot.

*****

Twenty-five years before, Don Bezahler was taking his annual stress test at New York Hospital—Cornell Medical Center.

"Suddenly the technician turned off the treadmill and brought me to another room. After sitting around a bit, somewhat baffled by the sudden drama, two cardiologists entered. What they told me was startling, I had a rather unique issue—a membrane in my aorta was creating something of an eddy with my blood—something called Sub-aortic Stenosis. And while I was told it wasn't currently critical, it might well create a grave situation in the future."

At the time there were only two surgeons (one from Boston the other from California) who specialized in Sub-aortic Stenosis and both refused to consider operating on Don. He was advised that in the future, if other issues should require heart surgery, at that time his Sub-aortic Stenosis would be dealt with.

A few years earlier, Don's medical condition equation got a bit dicey when Don, while dining with his wife, Suzanne, and some friends at a Mexican restaurant in Vermont, noticed that his right arm was swelling up—his watch a garrote on his wrist.

"I recall removing the watch as my arm continued to swell. Completely perplexed, I was ushered to a clinic, as there were no hospitals nearby in rural Vermont."

The brain trust at the clinic diagnosed the issue as a bee-sting or insect bite. Don was administered Benadryl. Not only did the swelling remain, but the following day Don's other arm took on the same symptoms. Something was seriously wrong.

Still in Vermont, Don went to a different clinic. A nurse/ practitioner (ironically named Mary), administered a blood test.

When Nurse Mary returned, she knew one thing; there was an anomaly in Don's blood. She couldn't diagnose it, and frankly wouldn't venture a guess. But she did advise that he look into it ASAP.

As the swelling ebbed, Don paid little attention to the situation or the advice of the medic. That is, until a few months later, while at 35,000 feet and thirty minutes out of Miami International Airport, Don found he couldn't speak and could barely breathe.

From his first-class seat, Don quickly penned a message to the steward explaining his dire situation. Within moments the plane's loudspeaker blared the pilots voice, asking, "Is there a doctor on board?" Three showed up!

Of the trio, one was a surgeon. Apparently, he outranked the rest and took over the situation. Having only the plane's medical kit at his disposal, the doctor administered an injection of Benadryl. He also, however, advised the cockpit that they must land without delay and that an ambulance must be on the tarmac at the ready. Don's throat was closing and it was a race against time.

The plane was given priority-landing status—an ambulance pulled up under the shadow of the plane's massive wing, and Don was taken out on a stretcher.

"Pan American Hospital was located five-minutes from the airport and so that's where I was taken. It was chaotic, the EMT guys were stating the situation was critical, the nurse was attempting to get air into my lungs while a doctor began shooting me up with steroids."

Don penned another missive, that his wife be called. When Suzanne arrived, Don wrote her a note requesting that she call Mary. To Suzanne's credit she did indeed make the call, however she refused Mary's overture to come to the hospital.

Don's life was saved. He spent the next two days at the hospital going through a barrage of tests, to no avail. His condition was baffling to say the least.

"I began visiting specialists in both Florida and New York and through that process I was advised of someone in West Virginia, an immunologist, who could only be approached through a fellow doctor's referral. Sadly, the effort was to no avail as the Virginia specialist took a pass."

Frustrated but undaunted, the enterprising Don decided to write directly to this "hot-shot Doc." He sent a three-page letter and included all his records, imploring the doctor to see him.

While waiting for a response from West Virginia, Don heard of another renowned immunologist at New York's Mount Sinai Hospital. And while she too passed, she did recommend an associate she felt would be a better fit considering Don's situation.

"I researched the suggested doctor—she was thirty-years old, which didn't strike a lot of confidence in me. Her name Paula Busse. With no options, I decided to at least meet with the 'kid.'"

After poring through his records and running Don through her own examination, Paula Busse told Don, with utter confidence, that she knew his issue—her diagnosis—Hereditary Angioedema.

"They say timing is everything. Well, let me tell you, not only was she spot on in her diagnosis but Hereditary Angioedema was her specialty, she'd just returned from testifying before the FDA advocating a new medicine specifically designed to deal with the disease!"

As if that wasn't endorsement enough, shortly thereafter Don received a call from the vaunted doc from West Virginia. Don's letter had won the day, the doctor agreed to see Don. However, when Don brought him up to speed regarding Paula Busse, the doctor told him not to bother coming, that "Busse was the best in the business."

Knowing that Don could be stricken at almost any given time, Dr. Busse arranged for him to carry a C1 inhibitor and needles and syringes at all times.

In layman's terms, Hereditary Angioedema is a genetic mutation. Without C1 inhibitor in his blood, any skin prick--even a cold or a deep bruise--can send the good white corpuscles into attack mode. Without the C1 inhibitor, however, the antibodies attack everything, including the victim's own tissue.

In early October 2017, during a routine cardio exam at Mount Sinai in Miami Beach, doctors found Don's calcification level had risen from moderate to severe. Shortly thereafter, Don was issued the two-year warning or go-under-the-knife alternative. We know what Don decided, and why, but here's the rub.

On November 3rd Don would undergo a pre-surgical procedure (cauterization) to determine any further damage to his heart, which might require a stent. While this may be protocol, Don's blood condition would certainly set off the chain reaction of the Hereditary Angioedema.

This potentially fatal situation could repeat itself on November 10, when Don would undergo minimally invasive heart surgery to remove the membrane from his aorta and receive his new aortic valve.

Needless to say, Dr. Busse and ace surgeon, Dr. Xydas, formulated a plan, but it was untested. Don would receive an infusion of C1 prior to the procedure, and one after. If all goes well, that scenario would repeat itself during the main surgery. It's a risk, but one Don was willing to take.

If this was a motion picture, this is the part where the music would be cued, and audience eyes would begin to tear up.

CHAPTER 17
EVERY SURGERY DESERVES A CELEBRATION

"'Tis better to have loved and lost, then never to have loved at all."
~ Alfred Lord Tennyson

November 2017—Pre-Surgery Feast at Hollywood Beach

Mary Mathis has prepared a traditional Thanksgiving feast—turkey, stuffing, mashed potatoes, and homemade pecan pie—the works.

It's Saturday, a week before Don's open-heart surgery was to take place and over two-weeks before the "official" Thanksgiving Day is to commence.

"You're doing this because you suspect this is my final Thanksgiving, isn't that right Mary? No more wishbones for Don Bezahler, isn't that it," Don joked.

"Actually, Pilgrim, we are celebrating Thanksgiving, 2017. And yes, it's a bit early, but only because on the actual date you'll be recovering in a hospital room at Mount Sinai in Miami!"

And such is the tête-à-tête of the twosome—the pair fondly referred to as 'MaryandDon', all one word—no last name required.

*****

Mary Mathis sat at the very round table where her husband, Don, had sat only two weeks prior. Don had spoken with great candor about his love for Mary, his concern of death and his upcoming open-heart surgery. She was talking about how Don will be home in a few short days since the operation was a smashing success.

"I had already lost two fiancées in operating rooms—one from a lung surgery, the other from a heart surgery—and these were young men in the prime of their lives. Obviously, I was a bit gun shy," Mary admitted.

This confirmed what Don had once said, that the key sticking point in their budding romance was their age difference, and Mary's fear of prematurely losing the man she loved.

"It was the proverbial fly in the ointment," Mary said, with a shrug and a slight smile. "I simply didn't want my heart broken. Of course, I was very much in love with Don, and so the thought of our age difference leaving me a lonely, grieving widow was, frankly, a frightening proposition. I wanted to grow old with Don!"

Ultimately, it was Alfred Lord Tennyson's "Tis better to have loved and lost," refrain that won the day, and of course 'MaryandDon' stuck it out and have been inseparable ever since.

What eventually won the day and assuaged Mary's fear of an octogenarian open-heart surgery was numbers—simple math.

"Meeting with Dr Xydas (Don's surgeon) was the turning point. Calmly and matter-of-factly, he explained that without the surgery the chance of mortality was 40 percent within 12-24 months. The risk of death during surgery was one percent, and the risk of death due to post-op complications was five percent. I didn't need to be Archimedes to do the math."

Of course, Don's HAE concern and how it would impact the operation, had been anyone's guess as the only previously documented, same-type situation, was a tonsillectomy performed on a much younger person.

"I took over the management program of the C1 Inhibitor. I spoke with his specialist, his cardiologist, his surgical team, the hospital administration, and with Bio RX, the manufacturer of Don's medicine (Berinert). I wanted to be sure there would be more than enough of the drug on hand—they were very accommodating. The hospital pharmacist on the other hand wasn't so much."

"While I wanted a supply on hand in Don's room at all times, I was met with resistance. The pharmacist demanded that this expensive substance stay in the pharmacy and he tried, to no avail, to assure me that someone on duty would have access at all times. There was no way in hell that scenario was going to fly—not on my watch!"

A compromise was eventually struck. The hospital provided a safe in Don's room where the medication would be stowed. Mary had won the day.

Mary reflected on the awkward build-up to the operation. How she and Don had to address final arrangements—had to be sure his business was in order, as it were.

"We were forced to have the 'Hard' discussion. One of the subjects was where Don wished to be buried. He had a plot in a cemetery in Mount Hebron, New York, where other family members were interred."

Don said, "I'm concerned that if I'm buried in New York you won't come to visit me!"

Mary answered, "Your body may be in New York, but your soul and your spirit will be with me!"

A solution was eventually reached, with a memorial garden planned—a plaque memorializing Don as well as the ashes of their past canine pets included. This would make daily "visits" possible!

Days before the slated surgery, everything was wrapped up, from health care surrogate, to power of attorney, to a final and proper will, in accordance with Don's wishes.

"You hate to seem maudlin but having all those affairs in order brought a great amount of peace of mind to the both of us," he said.

Don's son, David, arrived from Los Angeles on Wednesday. The threesome had dinner together and then headed out to the hospital on Thursday for pre-registration—the actual operation was slated for Friday morning.

"David and I sat in the chapel, where the surgical nurse would contact us every hour on the hour with updates," Mary said. "We received about five communiqués, and during that period the two of us became tighter than ever."

"When the surgery was complete, Dr. Xydas informed us that he was very pleased with the results, and an hour or so later, both David and I were allowed into Don's ICU room where we spoke soothing words of encouragement—hoping that Don could hear us or at least feel our presence."

David and Mary returned to the Polk Street pad planning on a celebratory supper at Billy's Stone Crab. And that's when Mary stumbled. Brushing off the pain, she hobbled over to Billy's with David in tow.

"I ordered ice for my foot before I ordered a glass of French Rosé for my frazzled nerves," Mary laughed with ease, her foot now in a walking boot. The stumble resulted in a slight fracture, which she did not get diagnosed until a week after the fall.

The following day, David, as arranged, went to Delray Beach to visit his mother, Don's first wife, Norma. Mary had asked David to find out from his Orthodox Jewish mother, the proper protocol in the event that things took a turn for the worse. Norma was happy to lend her knowledge of Jewish Law regarding such unpleasantries.

Even Suzanne, Don's second wife and the woman supplanted by Mary, sent Don her best wishes. Don's crisis seemed to pull all the players in his life together in a cacophony of civility.

The following day, when Mary went to visit Don, he resembled something of the Frankenstein monster.

"Don was attached to wires and tubes, a catheter, and all types of monitors and IV's, and while heavily sedated, he knew I was there. Taking my hand in his he whispered, 'I love you.'"

CHAPTER 18
TIME TO GO HOME

Don't piss off the patient, especially when he's a Dragon-Slayer...

December 3, 2017—Mount Sinai Medical Center, Miami Beach

Don Bezahler went in for his open-heart surgery on November 10, and it went off without a hitch.

"I was told that I would be returning home after 12 days--15 max, if there were issues—what a load," he said with a snort. "After 23 days of sucking fluid out of my lungs and me having moved into a private room, which by the way, cost me three hundred and fifty smackers a night—I finally said, 'To hell with you, I'm out of here!'"

To fully appreciate the stubborn continence of Don Bezahler, you must understand the man was never sick. For thirty-years, he never missed a single day of work. And other than the Hereditary Angioedema, diagnosed after visits to five hospitals and seven doctors—where Don would simply get his shot and be on his way—nothing rattled him, nothing kept him out of the line-up. That's just the way he is.

Despite the knowledge, for many years, that there was an anomaly in his main heart valve, Don never wavered, until he was finally told the jig was up, it was time to open him up or perhaps he could hang tight for a year, maybe two.

"So, there's fluid in my lungs and they have a tube inserted in my back sucking out the fluids, and I'm pissed because I'm used to being the one in control and now I have doctors and specialists and who-knows-what running around controlling my situation. And frankly, I'm feeling good, but I obey their yammering," Don said, recalling his frustration.

"Eventually, they pull the plug. They've gotten most of the fluid out and I'm ready for home-sweet-home, and then they tell me there is an issue with the viscosity of my blood. They say it needs to be somewhere between 2.5 and 3 and I'm testing at 1.65 or thereabouts. This blood issue has to do with clotting, and I get it, we don't want clots and we don't want a stroke or worse."

"So, each and every day at 4 p.m. they take blood. And each and every day it's the same story—I'm not hitting the mark. And while my blood wasn't clotting it was boiling!"

At this point in the movie, Don is footing the bill for that private room at $350 a night. And while Mount Sinai is one of the top hospitals in the world, it ain't the Plaza or the Carlyle or any of the luxury hotels Don has spent a life luxuriating in. He's pissed.

"I finally told them enough already. I'm out of here!" Don was released under the provision that he would have someone come to his home in Hollywood each day for blood thinning injections. He took the deal.

On January 4, 2018, Don was given a clean bill of health. No more restrictions. He can work, walk, fly—even drink his favorite champagne. And as a matter of fact, after he and his beloved Mary left the hospital, they dropped into Le Zoo, one of their favorite haunts, and imbibed on exactly that, $25 glasses of Champagne and a wonderful brunch.

"Mary and I had plans to travel to New York on the 11th of January and there was no stopping us. Finally, I felt back in control of my life."

There was still one hurdle, however. Upon being released from the hospital Don had a heart monitor inserted in his chest, the goal was to monitor over one million beats and track the possibility of arrhythmia.

"At 8 p.m. the following day, the day after our champagne celebration, the hospital calls—there's an issue with arrhythmia and they need me to come in to see another specialist. I told them I'd see him, but I wasn't about to listen to him!"

At this point Don is livid. There's a strong possibility that the variation in heartbeats is simply a reaction to the surgery. A natural side effect. Furthermore, the Hereditary Angioedema that was striking Don on a weekly basis is non-existent since the surgery. Don is not only in a state of repair; it seems he is better than ever!

"My bones were healing just fine, the holes in my chest as well. My vitals were perfect, blood pressure spot on—hell, I was gliding up and down the stairs of the house! And then this," he nearly yelled.

While Don scrapped the planned trip to New York, he refused to give it up for good, vowing to reschedule, or as he said it, "Come hell or high-water!"

CHAPTER 19
CAN'T KEEP A GOOD MAN DOWN

What if you gave a party and no one came. What if you lived a life and no one cared?"
~ Don Bezahler

April 20, 2018—15th Street Fisheries, Fort Lauderdale, FL

Don Bezahler and Mary Mathis used to visit this famed eatery in the fledgling days of their relationship. "Back then we'd enjoy the view, dine, imbibe, laugh, and then each go our separate ways—back to the existences that drove us together in the first place."

But on this April day, Don and Mary drove back to their Hollywood beachside home together, wearing sly smiles. You see, they'd planned a birthday bash for Mary. An excursion which would take them to Nice, Barcelona, and New York—this despite Don's recent open heart surgery.

"Regardless of the scene, Mary and I shall live-it-up until the final curtain drops," Don insisted.

WINTER

There comes a point in one's life when they might be asked to do some reflection, and to share the results of that soul-searching. Don called this "winter."

"It's difficult to reflect on a long-life, to collate your existence and experiences. And it's especially challenging and daunting to figure out where fall ends and winter begins," Don said quietly.

"Quite frankly, I never had much time for reflection or introspection. I was always on the go—never bored, never restless, and never sick. Perhaps it was my recent medical issue which provided me a sense of mortality, which in-turn demanded a good-long look in the mirror of my life."

And while Don embarked on this project prior to his diagnosis, the process became more urgent and revealing once vulnerability cast its graven shadow.

"I suddenly had to make important, life determining decisions. I could no longer count on tomorrow to stand in line and wait for a personal audience. I had to cut down on drinking, watch my diet, limit travel and exertion, and most importantly, tidy up my affairs."

Don began to question what type of legacy he'd leave behind—it seemed a seesaw battle. On the one hand there were many intimates--ex-wives and a son who had been disappointed in how he had conducted his life.

On the other hand, he had always provided for those

very same people. And after all, hadn't he and his son, David, and daughter in-law, Amber, patched up their differences and found fulfillment?

And, while Don outlived so many of his friends and associates, hadn't he the respect of the many folks he'd mentored and guided, both personally and professionally?

And, didn't many of his earlier detractors embrace the "new" Don that seemed to materialize after he met Mary—a more personable and compassionate version of the "Dragon Slayer"?

"The social media phenomenon of Facebook really became an eye opener. Of course, that was Mary's doing. She began posting some of my writings on her page, and the response was overwhelming," Don confided.

"These posts would garner 70-80 likes and comments, many from friends and acquaintances I'd long since forgotten. It made me realize I had made an impact, an impression, on so many people."

Don became deeply reflective and asked, as much to himself as anyone, "What if you gave a party and no one came? What if you lived a life and no one cared?"

He reminisced over a lecture he'd given in Israel some years ago. One he'd gone to great expense to host. "When I entered the hall, expecting a crowd, there was absolutely no one in attendance. I was crestfallen. How could I have so misjudged my relevancy? Suddenly, as if floodgates had burst, the space filled with hundreds of attendees."

"I've reached a place where, if no one shows up at my funeral, it won't matter a whit. What I am comfortable with is that I'm providing for so many people in my life. The most I can expect is to be thought of on occasion. Perhaps people will say, 'He was a hell-of-a-guy—someone who made an impression as a giving, caring, mentoring man.' I'd like to be remembered, not as the man I once was, but as the man I became."

Don added, "Whether I have one more day, or a year, or a decade, I'm content. I've made my peace and organized my affairs and have set in place a protective embrace around those I love."

He recently asked Mary, with genuine concern, "How will you handle things when I'm gone?" Mary responded, "I'll be fine. I learned from a master. But do me a favor Don, stick around for a while!"

"I enter the winter of my life with dignity and self-respect. I can walk with my head held high," Don emphasized.

Don's legacy is indeed a twist on James Bond's vaunted martini—a life stirred not shaken!

CHAPTER 20
SHAKEDOWNS, SIT-DOWNS, VOODOO DOLLS & THE MOB

"Memories of an unusual career"

STORY I

In 1963 Don Bezahler was between wife number one and wife number two—living and practicing law in New York City. One of Don's clients had loaned a road-builder from British Guiana $125,000. As collateral, the lender received British Guiana bonds. While the bonds had a face value of $1 million, the actual value was projected to be around the $125,000 mark—the reason for the discrepancy was because, at the time, it was thought the government would not honor the bonds at full value.

As fate would have it, just about the time the road-builder defaulted on the loan, the British government announced forthcoming plans to grant full independence to their Caribbean colony.

"As a result of Britain's intentions, the Guianese would

be forced to pay the bonds in full or risk losing their credit rating—jeopardizing any future funding from the United States. Suddenly, my client was sitting on a cool million!"

Heeding Don's advice, the client forgave the loan on the default and held onto the bonds. That's when the road-builder started a lawsuit in British Guiana. His proposition was that he pays back the initial $125,000 and keeps the bonds for himself.

And off Don went to British Guiana.

"At the time, the Premier was a communist named Cheddi Jagan, someone who would most likely not be sympathetic to my clients cause. It would be an uphill battle," Don recalled.

"I was advised to make inroads with the Attorney General. It was also recommended that I bring onboard both an Indian and African attorney, the two races which best represented the populous and who could assist navigating the old-fashioned, British-style court system—think wigs and robes ala King George III."

Don made inroads with the attorney general (who was, in fact, of Indian descent). "I recall being invited to the AG's mother's home for afternoon tea. The woman plied me with food. I casually commented she reminded me of an old Jewish mother. It turned out that her mother was actually Jewish. You might say we hit it off."

The AG's sister was also present—an athletically built beauty who seemed keen on Don. "I took advantage of the situation. I figured it couldn't hurt to start dating. What I didn't know was that in their culture, after a fifth date you were essentially stating your courting intentions—something of a commitment to marriage. I couldn't afford to alienate the gal and family, so I played along for the sake of the case."

The trial went on for a couple of weeks. And not surprisingly, with corruption rampant, Don lost. But that wasn't the end of it.

"In accordance with their court system, we had the right to bring the case to the Caribbean Court of Appeals. Furthermore, if we lost there, we could wind up before the Privy Council of Britain. In the long run we weren't going to lose, as ultimately we'd be far from the kangaroo court atmosphere where the original case was tried."

Apparently, the plaintiff knew what Don knew, and therefore was amicable to sit down and deal with the New York sharpshooter.

"We kept the bonds, I paid him 100k, and we walked away 900k richer!"

During the trial, Don was ensconced in a local hotel, and the conditions were insufferable. "Once the sun went down, the rats came out in droves. So, each weekend my client would fly me to Trinidad to stay with him and his wife at the Hilton—a five-star hotel. I relished these weekend getaways."

Since the client and his wife had taken a suite, there was a room for Don to occupy. "One evening, nearing the end of the trial, my client told me that the two of us were going to meet with some Trinidad government mucky-mucks. This guy was always up to something, the consummate player."

"In any event, we wound up at a strip-club where booze flowed liberally. At some point, one of the dancers took me on-stage, and while I tried to resist, our guests and my host encouraged me along—what's a guy to do?"

Don went onstage, where he was summarily undressed down to his skivvies. He accepted an offer to shower and freshen up before returning to his tablemates. "That was one memorable shower, it was located in the girl's dressing room and I wasn't alone under the spray!"

Don wasn't alone in the shower or afterwards, as one particularly fetching femme invited him back to her place for a little extracurricular activity. "I got back to the suite around 3 a.m., only to find my client's wife waiting and worried. Apparently he hadn't returned—it was awkward to say the least."

The good-time-Charlie eventually arrived back at the suite at 5:30 a.m., and needless to say, 'the shit-hit-the-fan.'

Don was on a flight for Guiana early the next morning.

When the deal was sealed, Don returned to New York. But not everyone who was left behind was happy. The jilted sister of the AG was crestfallen. It wasn't long before Don began receiving packages with pin stuck voodoo dolls.

Then another letter arrived stating the gals sister was coming to New York to set things right. "I had to get out of this situation. My plan was to seduce the visiting sister, which would prove that I was nothing more than a cad, someone to be avoided, not betrothed to."

The plan worked—both sisters were happy to wash their hands of the entire, sordid situation.

A case won; a bullet dodged.

STORY II

Don Bezahler was representing a client with a shady past—rumored to be mob connected. And while the client owned a "legitimate" company, he'd never held a stockholders meeting. Apparently there were some rumblings, and so a meeting was hastily organized in Atlantic City, of all places.

"The client not only requested that I attend the meeting, but he demanded I conduct it. "It went off without a hitch. Everyone was happy and my client couldn't thank me enough."

That evening, a celebratory party was held at the Sahara. "This guy invited every gal in town—from showgirls to coat-checks, from waitresses to hookers.

"I was married to Suzanne at the time and we had something of a system in place for when I was on the road. I would call her each evening at 11 p.m. sharp." Don left the party and was back in his hotel room when he made the call to his wife.

"Just as I was getting ready to hit-the-sack there was a knock at my door. I opened it and was greeted with the visage of a pair of very attractive and seductively-clad twins. They explained that they had been sent to Don Bezahler as a present for 'a job well done.'"

While certainly tempted, Don wasn't biting. There was no way he'd allow himself to give leverage to a wise guy—even if he was a client. "I'd gone up to 'America's Playground' with an associate who was staying two-doors down from me. I explained to the tantalizing twins that I wasn't Don Bezahler, that he was staying in a room just down the hall. The girls headed off for their prey!"

"We were booked to return the following morning, only my associate wasn't budging. He said, 'Don, I can't thank you enough. I had the most incredible time ever last night. I'm not leaving!' I suspect I'd created, a win—win—win situation."

STORY III

Another of Don's clients was a real-estate developer who was having problems with trash collections at his New Jersey properties. Apparently, the mob, whom it was rumored, ran the "carting" racket, wanted to be greased for their services, above and beyond the standard fee.

Don noted, "My client was willing to pay, only not the amount of the shake-down. In any event, he asked me to intervene and a sit-down was arranged at a private room in the legendary downtown Manhattan restaurant, F.Illi Ponte."

{*Author's Note: According to Wikipedia, the restaurant was owned by 'Frank Angelo Ponte, an American mobster active in the Genovese family's carting rackets.*}

"So here we are, a couple of nice Jewish boys, seated at a table full of heavy-hitters. We discussed the issue for an hour. I explained my client's position. They offered compromise conditions. A deal was reached and we shook on it. My client never had the deal rescinded or altered in any way."

Now that's trash talk!

STORY IV

Don had a client from California. This gentleman has a son with a penchant for baking exceptional cookies.

"My client requested that I find a spot in Manhattan for his son to open a bakery and restaurant. I found a great location on 2nd Avenue in the 50's. I negotiated the lease and construction began. The problem was that every damn night the place was vandalized—rocks through windows, the works."

It wasn't long before Don got the message. There happened to be a cookie store right around the corner on 53rd between 2nd and 3rd. Apparently, the place was a mob front— more laundering than baking was being done. Competition could cut into the bottom line, and the goodfellas weren't going for that scenario. A sit-down ensued.

"They made me an offer I couldn't refuse. 'Buy our cookie shop for a set sum, otherwise your endeavor will never see the light of day!'" In typical Don Bezahler style, he arranged the sale, and then he added the twist. He turned the existing space into a massively successful wholesale operation, selling baked goodies to eateries throughout New York, New Jersey, and Connecticut. The original retail restaurant/bakery opened in its initial spot.

All parties *lived* happily ever after!

CHAPTER 21
DINNER'S ON DON

"Why should I foot a bill for a feast prepared by and eaten by the owner...the manager...the chef, and Mary and Don?"

August 2014—Hudson Valley, NY

You might say Mary Mathis is quirky and therefore the perfect foil to Don "The Dragon Slayer" Bezahler.

Now you must understand, Don was a world-traveler (whether business or pleasure) and always stayed in massive suites at 5-star hotels wherever he was.

Mary, no slouch herself in the globetrotting gamut, had, shall we say, perhaps more daring or unconventional tastes when it came to accommodations.

So, when the summer of 2014 rolled around and it seemed the couple would once again stay at their friend's pastoral Vermont home, why Mary had other ideas.

With Alice, their trusty but aged, golden retriever in tow and preparing for their annual summer jaunt, Mary pitched a sidetrack scenario. She'd found Audrey's, a quaint, pet-friendly, farmhouse B&B (circa 1740) in Wallkill, New York, based at the foot of Shawangunk Ridge in the Hudson Valley.

When they arrived, it was easier to get their golden

retriever, Alice out of the car than it was Don, but Don finally agreed to give it a look-see. He did find it charming, but there were issues. The first was there were no suites available on the ground floor (a lesbian couple on their honeymoon had the one suite downstairs), which meant a room on the second floor.

The problem, however, was that poor old Alice was unable to navigate the tight and narrow stairway to the second floor. They were, nonetheless, charmed by the manager's insistence that she would sleep with the dog in the parlor.

Fortunately, another couple overheard the unfolding imbroglio. The husband happened to be a hefty and hearty Cuban and he offered Mary and Don the task of hoisting Alice up the stairs when needed. Even Don had to admit, while a bit unconventional the service at Audrey's rivaled that of the Ritz.

Settled in for their three-night stay, the couple (and Alice) acclimated quickly. The natural swimming pond was grand, the backyard a veritable jungle playground for dogs to romp, an eclectic array of guests, and the best breakfast ever.

Yes, it was those multiple-course breakfasts with the seasonal fruits and sustainable food in the cozy nook of a dining room that got Mary thinking.

'What on earth could she be up to?' Don could only wonder when Mary returned from a tour of the kitchen after an enchanting conversation with the chef and that look in her eye.

Now, there's not a lot of dining options at the foot of

Shawangunk Ridge, and so, other than the delightful daily breakfasts, quality food was scarce and that's what prompted Mary to suggest that they host a dinner party at Audrey's.

Don, of course, was incredulous. He couldn't quite fathom why he should foot the bill for a feast prepared by and eaten by the owners, the manager and her husband, and the chef and his wife, while he was already paying a fairly hefty nightly tag for the room as it were.

But the "Dragon Slayer" had met his match, and he knew that when he married Mary in the first place, with spontaneity being so much of her charm. So Don agreed, and Mary ran off to discuss the menu with the powers that be.

What a lively and scrumptious soiree it was—canapés and hors d'oeuvres in the parlor—with aperitifs galore. Then the multi-course meal in the dining room, and, of course, after-dinner drinks in abundance. The evening went deep into the wee hours of the morning.

Notwithstanding the $750 tab, all in all it was a glorious and delightful evening 'MaryandDon' style...

DINNER AT AUDREY'S FARMHOUSE
Sunday, August 17, 2014

Assorted Sprout Creek Farm Cheeses with local honeycomb

Fresh figs

San Francisco sourdough bread

Bib lettuce with mixed greens, fresh peaches, Gorgonzola cheese, golden beets, candied pecans, croutons, olive oil drizzle

Homemade porcini mushroom ravioli in a porcini white truffle broth with shards of Asagio cheese

Pan-seared Atlantic halibut with roasted white turnip, rice pilaf with Brunoise vegetables, and roasted hearts of palm

Pan-seared double-cut lamb chops with white truffle paste, fingerling potatoes and roasted white turnips

Cabernet poached pears and roasted almond gelato with chocolate. Espresso mint glaze and homemade biscotti.

Coffee

EPILOGUE

It is now April 2020. Mary and Don celebrated their ninth wedding anniversary and Don is celebrating his 88th birthday tomorrow.

They are ensconced in their beautiful new apartment in Naples, Florida. At the ripe old age of 87, Don and Mary decided they needed a change, and, on a lark, purchased a new 4,000 square foot apartment in Cap Ferrat in Pelican Bay.

They knew not a soul in Naples, except for the real estate brokers who sold them the apartment.

Their new adventure started after they completed furnishing the new digs, and they started moving in at the end of the summer of 2019. Readers will recall that they spent three years and a fortune re-doing their home in Hollywood, Florida, but that did not deter the vagabonds who now have to take care of three homes. Luckily, the drive between Hollywood and Naples is only two hours.

Little did they know what nature had in store for them. It was easy to make friends in Naples, and Mary and Don flourished in their new surroundings. Don would fly back and forth between Naples and Manhattan, since he was still consulting with the Goldman family in Manhattan. Life could not have been happier for the lovebirds. People were friendly, restaurants were great, and both were feeling at peace with the world. On March 1st they rented out the beach house in Hollywood.

Whoever heard of the Corona Virus, and the Pandemic that began taking hold in March 2020? Suddenly, no restaurants, no visits with friends, and no mingling with neighbors in the building or community. Don was worried about Mary, and Mary was worried, too much so, about Don. Don has a very rare, life threatening, autoimmune condition, and every day the TV was cautioning about keeping such persons safe.

Don's activities were limited to reading, taking Asia, their wonderful golden retriever, on walks, watching TV, and trying to complete this biography.

Mary was charged with the tasks of doing everything else. What else was there? Shopping, cleaning, cooking, worrying about Don, and taking care of her own business. Each task was difficult in the age of the Pandemic. It looks as if life should return to something close to normal sometime soon, when our brave couple plan to return to Manhattan for the summer months.

Don quips, "Neither Don nor Mary can wait for Don to get out of the house and return to the office. In all seriousness we were lucky to move when we did, since this is just about the safest place we can be at this time."

Life, and the beat goes on.